The Adopter's Handbook on
Therapy

GETTING THE BEST
FOR YOUR CHILD

Eileen Fursland

coramBAAF
ADOPTION & FOSTERING ACADEMY

Published by
CoramBAAF Adoption and Fostering Academy
41 Brunswick Square
London WC1N 1AZ
www.corambaaf.org.uk

Coram Academy Limited, registered as a company limited by guarantee in England and Wales number 9697712, part of the Coram group, charity number 312278

British Library Cataloguing in Publication Data
A catalogue record for this book is available from the British Library

ISBN 978 1 910039 49 6

Project management by Shaila Shah, Director of Publications, CoramBAAF
Designed by Helen Joubert Design
Printed in Great Britain by The Lavenham Press

Trade distribution by Turnaround Publisher Services, Unit 3, Olympia Trading Estate, Coburg Road, London N22 6TZ

Contents

Acknowledgements

I'd like to thank all those people and organisations whose knowledge, experience and work I have been able to draw on to compile this guide.

John Simmonds OBE, Director of Policy, Research and Development, CoramBAAF Adoption and Fostering Academy, provided valuable input, as did Gail Simmonds, a counsellor. Thank you to CoramBAAF's Director of Publications, Shaila Shah, for commissioning the guide and bringing it to publication and to Jo Francis, editor at CoramBAAF, for her input.

I am grateful to those who kindly gave their permission for us to quote their insightful views on adoption and adoption support: Al Coates, Gareth Marr and Sally Donovan; and the anonymous writers who have shared their personal accounts of what it's like to need support and what has helped them: Mending Mum, FASD Mum, Mo and Bro, the two adoptive dads who write the blog 'Our Journey Through Adoption', frogotter, and the adopted teenager who wrote her story for the AT-iD website. Every effort has been made to trace copyright holders and to obtain their permission for the use of copyright material. We apologise for any errors or omissions and would be grateful if notified of any corrections that should be incorporated in future reprints or editions of this book.

About the author

Eileen Fursland is a freelance writer specialising in issues affecting children and young people. She has written extensively for BAAF (now CoramBAAF) on a number of publications since 2002, as well as for a range of magazines and national newspapers and other organisations.

Eileen's publications for BAAF include the training course *Preparing to Adopt* (she wrote the first edition in 2002 with a working party from BAAF which devised the course, and the fourth edition, 2014, with Nicky Probert and Elaine Dibben); her books *Facing up to Facebook* (second edition 2013); *Social Networking and Contact* (2010); *Foster Care and Social Networking* (2011); *Social Networking and You* (2011); and *Ten Top Tips on Supporting Education*, with Kate Cairns and Chris Stanway. In earlier collaborations with Kate Cairns, she co-wrote BAAF's training programmes, *Trauma and Recovery*; *Safer Caring*; *Building Identity*; and *Transitions and Endings*. Eileen also provides training sessions on the implications of social networking for adoption and fostering and how to manage the challenges it poses (www.create-and-communicate.com).

Narratives by adoptive parents, picture books for children and guides for direct work with children

Introduction

Adopted children can be loving, affectionate, happy, clever, funny, mischievous and adorable. They can bring joy to their adoptive parents and make their lives complete.

But this is a book about adoption support. So it looks at what can be done for the children who can only manage to be some of those things, some of the time.

Adoption isn't a "happy ending". It's a new beginning, and for the child it's the start of a journey to reach his or her full potential with the support of a loving family.

For the child, putting the past behind them isn't always easy. The legacy of their early experiences (and for some, damage suffered before they were born) leaves many adopted children fragile, wary, anxious, depressed, angry, emotionally volatile, unable to make sense of their lives and their identity, and struggling to make healthy relationships. How can they be supported to get to a calmer and happier place? And what can be done to help the adoptive parents who often bear the brunt when their children make their pain felt, loud and clear?

> We live on planet adoption. Our lives are so very distinct to other parents. We applaud when our child cries...because it's rare that they've trusted us enough to show emotion. We are disappointed and distressed as the leader says all our son did at Scout camp were the rubbish jobs no-one else wanted. This is upsetting because we know that the reason he selected those roles is because he feels utterly worthless. When your daughter refuses school and swears, kicks you and punches a hole in the wall you think that it's a run-of-the-mill morning and your greatest achievement is to be able to step out of the drama and drink a cup of coffee while it's still hot.

(Jenni B Lacey, The POTATO Group (Parents of Traumatised Adopted Teens Organisation))

If you are reading this book, chances are you are an adoptive parent. And as an adoptive parent, you will have read the books (and possibly also the blogs and the tweets); been on the preparation course; spent more hours than you care to remember talking to social workers; and bonded and, sometimes, commiserated with other adopters over the challenges of life with your adopted children. In other words, you have been there, done that and got the T-shirt.

So you will already know about the importance of attachment and about what it means for a child when that initial bond never seems to form, or when it appears to be disrupted or broken. You'll have thought about what it does to a baby or young child's emotional development when no caring adult consistently responds to their cries or their attempts to "reach out" to those around them. You'll realise how a child's sense of trust and security is damaged if adults have failed to provide for his basic needs and if he has witnessed – or experienced – violence and abuse, lived with an unpredictable or frightening adult or repeatedly been moved from one carer to another. You'll be familiar with the effects of alcohol or substance abuse in pregnancy on a developing baby's brain. You'll be only too well aware that trauma can have long-term consequences for a child's physiological, social, emotional and behavioural development.

As an adoptive parent, you may also have come to recognise that when it comes to healing these children, love is not always enough. A child can continue to have difficulties for years, even when he is now living in a safe and loving home with caring parents who are committed to him. Or he may have a calm and happy childhood but then become a troubled and angry teenager.

The legacy of abuse and neglect in a child's early life can last for years, sometimes even a lifetime. Some children avoid emotional intimacy and you can't get near them. Some struggle to form relationships with siblings and friends too. A child whose early life was marked by stress and trauma may be sad, fearful and withdrawn. He may be controlling, quick to have outbursts of rage, bouncing off the walls, impulsive, stressed, unable to sit still, follow instructions or "behave". His physiological system may be on "high alert" for danger, perceiving threats where there are none. He may react to everyday events in unexpected ways that leave adults baffled. His emotions may be volatile and extreme, or he may seem dissociated or "cut off" from his environment and those around him. As they get older, some turn to self-harm or substance abuse to try and blot out their pain.

The need for adoption support

As has been set out above, a significant proportion of adopters find life is not at all easy. Professor Julie Selwyn and her colleagues from the Hadley Centre for Adoption and Foster Care Studies at the University of Bristol carried out a research study called *Beyond the Adoption Order,* the first national study on adoption disruption. They found that the majority of adopters questioned in the study described the adoptions as either "going well" or with "highs and lows, but mainly highs". But as many as 21–25 per cent of adopters described family life as difficult, while 8–9 per cent of the young people had left home under the age of 18 years.

> ...many adopters took the opportunity to give more detail on the difficulties their children were struggling with, such as attention deficit hyperactivity disorder (ADHD), post-traumatic stress disorder (PTSD), obsessive compulsive disorder (OCD), autistic spectrum disorders (ASD), foetal alcohol spectrum disorders (FASD), developmental trauma, learning difficulties, aggression, difficulties in managing anger, and a lack of empathy. Inadequate support and lack of information were common themes that ran through adopters' comments.

(Selwyn *et al*, 2015, pp58-9)

Professor Selwyn and her colleagues lifted the lid on child-to-parent violence in adoptive families in a way that had not been seen before. They found a significant number of families where the adoption had not broken down but the family was nonetheless under severe stress due to the extremely challenging and disturbing behaviour of the adopted child.

> Many parents described feeling vulnerable and frightened by their child's behaviour. Some parents could not bear to be alone at home with their child for fear of being physically attacked, bullied or dominated.

(Selwyn *et al*, 2015, p123)

Some adopters experienced extreme stress, mental health problems and marital breakdown as well as the risk of the child having to move out of the family home.

But despite these serious difficulties, parents often could not get the help they needed.

> Parents described arguments between the placing and receiving local authority and between children's services, education and health authorities about where responsibility for support lay. Parents said that agencies had "passed the buck"...
>
> Assessments that recommended expensive support packages were often denied...Some parents had been on "waiting lists" for post-adoption support, as both children's services and CAMHS (child and adolescent mental health services) were short-staffed. Even when local authorities

provided therapeutic services, they were usually time-limited (about six sessions) and/or provided many miles away from the family's home...

Many children had complex and overlapping needs that did not fit the tight criteria demanded for intervention by agencies.

(Selwyn *et al*, 2015, pp171-2)

Some adopters felt that no-one was listening when they did ask for help or that, instead of being given support, they were made to feel that it was their parenting that was at fault.

The majority of parents were critical of the support provided, of unhelpful advice and of the failure to provide appropriate services when needed... Parents wanted a service delivered by professionals who understood the complex and overlapping difficulties shown by adopted children.

(Selwyn *et al*, 2015, p244)

There is no excuse for inadequate support for adopters who have taken on the monumental task of parenting children who have had the most difficult starts imaginable.

Adopted children need an enhanced type of parenting, parenting that recognises and accommodates their needs, "fills in the gaps" of their early development, promotes their recovery, and helps them to learn to trust and to form a bond with their adoptive parents. And parents need help in managing the unique stresses of living with a child with a wide range of known and maybe unknown difficulties.

Adopters may have had the opportunity to attend one of the various training courses on "therapeutic parenting" that help adoptive parents to better understand the reasons behind their child's complex behaviour and how they might develop approaches that help manage this.

But as well as these and other types of support offered to adoptive parents, many adopted children need therapeutic help from mental health specialists and therapists who understand the range of possible issues and their underlying causes.

Getting effective help, at the right time, can make a huge difference for adopted children and their families. The Place2B, a charity that provides counselling in schools, states that:

A wealth of evidence points to a significant need for early mental health support...Children are less likely to suffer from serious mental health difficulties if they receive support at an early age...

Growing evidence indicates that promoting positive mental health also improves a range of positive school outcomes, including enhanced academic progress, better attendance and lower exclusion rates.

The right kind of help, at the right time, can mean that a child feels calmer and happier, is able to bond with their adoptive parents, and functions better at home and at school – which can mean a more harmonious family life, better educational achievement, improved life chances and a brighter future. In cases where the strain on the family has been extreme, it can make the difference between keeping the family together, and the child or young person having to leave and live away from home.

When adoptive families approach local authorities for help for their child, there is a statutory obligation to carry out an assessment of the child's support needs. However, there is no corresponding duty on the local authority to actually provide the services to meet the needs identified through the assessment. As *The Adoption Passport: A support guide for adopters* (First4Adoption, 2015) makes clear:

Every adopter is entitled to an assessment of their adoption support needs, but local authorities do not have to provide support in response to an assessment. Which services you are able to access will depend on your circumstances. Local authorities are now required by law to tell adopters about adoption support services and their right to an assessment.

When adoption support is lacking

While some adopters are given excellent long-term support from their adoption agency, for others the support has fallen far short of what they need. As outlined above, adopters have had to battle with the authorities to get help for their children; waiting lists have been long and money short.

With some adopted children, as they get older their difficult behaviour escalates and their families reach crisis point. It is shocking to hear that desperate parents asking for respite care to give them and their adopted teenager some time away from daily confrontations have been told that the only way to access respite care is to have the child taken back into the care system.

The first step in getting support was for professionals to acknowledge that there was a problem, and, for most adoptive parents, this was not easily achieved. Many parents spoke about the battles they had to get support.

(Selwyn *et al*, 2015, p170)

A survey carried out by Adoption UK in 2012 (Pennington, 2012) found that 61 per cent of adoptive parents stated the need for therapeutic services but only 28 per cent of their agencies provided this support. Eighty-one per cent of adoptive parents who were assessed said their support needs were identified, but only 31 per cent were given, in full, the services that they had been identified as needing.

Everyone hopes that the Adoption Support Fund, launched across England in May 2015 (see Section 1), will turn things around. Although Section 1 discusses the Adoption Support Fund, which is available only in England, the focus of this book is on therapeutic interventions for the child as well as therapeutic parenting approaches for adoptive parents, many of which are available in different parts of the UK.

What is needed?

In 2013 Coram and Barnardo's published a report looking at adoption and what's needed to make adoptive placements that last and don't break down. They talked about the key role of post-placement support. They looked at what works.

There is evidence (McNeish and Scott, 2013) that doing the following things will help sustain adoptive placements:

- *Assume that all late adopted children and their adoptive families are likely to need a range of support for emotional and behavioural difficulties at some stage.*

- *Develop a comprehensive support plan as soon as a match has been made (including financial support where appropriate).*

- *Provide training and preparation for adopters that helps them understand troubled children's behaviour and gives them the skills to promote attachment and resilience.*

- *Provide coaching around the challenges of the particular child and the parenting strategies that may be helpful.*

- *Provide evidence-based parenting programmes for adopters of children with emotional and behavioural problems.*

- *Match new adopters with mentors who are experienced adopters with relevant experience, e.g. adopting a sibling group or a child with a different ethnic background.*

- *Include in the support plan strategies for addressing cultural identity.*

- *Provide ongoing and reliable support, which can be particularly critical for sustaining placements for disabled children where there may be a need for guaranteed breaks, co-ordination of support services, support into adulthood and access to specialist help.*

- *Ensure that contact arrangements with birth family members do not undermine the child's sense of belonging and permanence in their adoptive or foster family.*

However, even with the existence of the Adoption Support Fund, it is likely that the impact of austerity through reduced spending by local authorities on children's services will affect at least some of the things on this list, such as the availability of short breaks for children with disabilities. Respite care was a big gap identified in the Adoption UK survey (Pennington, 2012) – but the Every Disabled Child Matters campaign reported that over half of local authorities have cut spending on short breaks since 2011–12 and that families say it is more difficult to access short breaks.

For some adopted children with serious and challenging behaviour problems, individual or family-based therapy soon after the child is placed or perhaps years later is needed in addition to some or all of the items on the list above.

Apart from actually providing the services, what else would adopters like to see from their adoption support services?

Adoptive father, social worker and member of the Adoption Support Expert Advisory Group Al Coates argues for better support for adopters. He wrote the following online blog:

> *I had a thought, I should write an adopters' charter. Then I thought, I'm sure that I've read one somewhere. So, after a little Googling I discovered a charter produced by the Department for Education in 2011... Surprisingly, or not, there's not one mention of post adoption support. I honestly don't know what to say about that.*

> *So I've written my own little charter, an Adoption Support Charter.*

Adoption Support Charter

As an Adoption Support Service:
1. *We commit to being available and if not, get back to you promptly.*
2. *We commit to listening.*
3. *We commit to being honest and keeping you informed.*
4. *We commit to supporting parents to support their children.*
5. *We commit to show empathy and compassion.*
6. *We commit to offering emotional support and advice.*
7. *We commit to being honest about what we can and can't do.*
8. *We commit to work in partnership with you.*
9. *We commit to advocate for you, two voices are louder than one, and signpost you to appropriate professionals, services and training.*
10. *We commit to employing social workers with appropriate interpersonal skills and appropriate knowledge and giving them the time and resources to support families.*

As Adopters:
1. *We commit to not waiting until we are desperate or in crisis before we contact you.*
2. *We commit to listening.*
3. *We commit to working collaboratively with you.*
4. *We commit to being honest.*

What interests me is that often the stuff that can make the biggest impact has limited cost. The principles of respect, kindness, gentleness, encouragement and availability, these are the things that can make all the difference. We all know that resources are under ever more strain but the foundations of all post-adoption services should be on these, or similar, principles.

We could debate the specifics of the service and we should, but I'd like to see the kind of things I've listed as a start.

I often hear 'there was no money for services but my social worker was great and really helped'. I also hear 'my social worker made me feel like I was the problem, I'd rather not have him/her in the house'.

That is a shame on my profession.

(www. alcoates.co.uk/2015/09/an-adoption-support-charter.html)

How this guide is structured

- **Section 1, *Adoption support***, outlines various different types of adoption support, in particular the Adoption Support Fund and how it works.

- **Section 2, *About therapy***, looks at what therapy is, the possible drawbacks and questions of evidence and effectiveness.

- **Section 3, *Therapies and therapeutic parenting support***, covers a number of different therapies that can be helpful for adopted children and families. For each type of therapy we give a brief outline of the core principles, the history, what the therapy involves and what form the sessions are likely to take. This section is organised by type of therapy rather than by the condition or type of problem children may have. It covers individual therapies, therapies for parents and children together, and courses for groups of adoptive parents in how to parent children using an understanding of attachment theory and the neurobiology of trauma.

- **Section 4, *Finding a therapist who is right for your child***, outlines what to look for in a therapist and questions adopters might want to ask. It also provides a list of useful websites.

- **Section 5, *Personal accounts***, provides some blogs and personal stories about adopters' experiences of different types of support and therapy for them and their children. Every effort has been made to contact these contributors for permission to reprint their pieces; in most cases we have been successful and thank them for their kind permission.

SECTION 1
Adoption support

Support for adoptive parents comes from many different places. Adopters should, in an ideal world, get support from well-informed social workers, their adoption agencies, their child's school, GP, health and medical services, friends and members of their wider family. Adopters help each other too (see *Peer support*, below).

Many adoption agencies run workshops, training courses and regular support groups for adoptive parents and sometimes their children and teenagers. In addition, some specialised adoption support agencies provide more intensive support and interventions for families in crisis.

There are plenty of websites, videos and books for anyone who wants to learn more about childhood trauma and parenting a traumatised child. Well-known authors and speakers (from the US, the UK and elsewhere) who are specialists in attachment and trauma theory and translating this into effective practice with families speak at events, courses and conferences for adoptive parents.

There are also psychological therapies for adopted children and their families, which are the main focus of this book (outlined in Section 3). Many of these therapies qualify for funding in England using the Adoption Support Fund (pp13–23) where an assessment has indicated that a child or family would benefit.

Peer support

There is a wealth of groups that bring together adopters – both online and in the real world – to support each other and many of these are led by adopters.

Adoption UK

Adoption UK has a membership of over 10,000 adopters, prospective adopters and foster carers. Members can meet both online in the discussion forum and offline in local support groups to share the challenges and rewards of adoptive

1

parenting. Adoption UK also runs parenting courses led by adopters, as well as other events such as conferences.
www.adoptionuk.org

Adoption Link

Run by adopters, Adoption Link is a matching site – profiles of children awaiting adoption can be searched by prospective adopters and their social workers, and prospective adopters' profiles can be searched by family-finding social workers. In addition, Adoption Link is a safe and free online space for families to build their support network by finding others they can chat to or meet at events. Adopters can also use the playdate-finder to find and meet up with other adoptive families living nearby who have similar-aged children.
www.adoptionlink.co.uk

New Family Social

The only UK charity led by LGBT (lesbian, gay, bisexual, transgender) adopters and foster carers, it aims to provide a safe social network for its members, who number over 1,000 households. As well as its website with blogs and message boards, it has 16 active regional groups and organises national events for families to meet up and for children to make friends with others who also have LGBT adoptive parents or foster carers. 'NFS members can form strong, informal support networks. Smaller get-togethers, dinners, play dates and outings happen all the time,' says NFS.
www.newfamilysocial.org.uk

The Potato Group (Parents of Traumatised Adopted Teens Organisation)

The Potato Group describes itself as 'a peer-based service for families who are host to teenagers who hurt' and says it aims to 'help them access support, information, resources and friendship from people who are living it and truly understand'. Its members are parents of around 300 adopted teenagers from all over the UK.
www.thepotatogroup.org.uk

The Single Adopters Network

Set up by a single adoptive mother, Sarah Fisher, for other single adopters, this is 'a space for them to meet and support each other, in a friendly, non-judgemental environment'. It has an online discussion group, a secure forum where single adopters can ask for and offer help and advice, and (paid-for) coaching from Fisher herself.

www.singleadoptersnetwork.com

The Adoption Social

This online community blog and support network was founded and is hosted by two adoptive mums, Vicki and Sarah. It collects together blogs written by adopters (and adoptees, birth mothers and others) who wish to share their thoughts and experiences and read those of others. The Adoption Social also hosts Twitter chats where you can join in a conversation with other tweeters and exchange views on various aspects of adoption.

www.theadoptionsocial.com

The Open Nest

The Open Nest is a unique place founded and run by adoptive mother Amanda Boorman and her team. This charity is based in Whitby, North Yorkshire, and offers post-adoption peer support, advice, respite holidays and short breaks with activities for children, and training in a therapeutic environment. Adoptive families can stay at the camp, and parents can relax or take part in training while children have fun with other adopted children.

www.theopennest.co.uk

Growing Together

A new group for new adopters, Growing Together is an adopter-led group for those who are getting to know their new children, whether they are approaching matching panel, or are in the first months or years of placement.

www.linkmaker.co.uk.

We are Family

We are Family adoption support community runs four regular local groups in and around Greater London.

https://wearefamilyadoption.wordpress.com

Other groups

There are also many support groups for parents of children with specific conditions, such as foetal alcohol spectrum disorders. See Section 5 for an account of one adoptive mother's first visit to her local support group.

And then there's Twitter and blogging…

There's a whole thriving and supportive adoption community to be found on Twitter and in the "blogosphere", where adopters find other like-minded adopters via their tweets and blogs about adoption. Here you can share questions and tips on caring for your children (and yourself), moral support, campaigning for change, practical information, observations about the highs and lows of adoptive family life and, when needed, online "hugs" from Twitter friends.

The Adoption Support Fund

Adoption support: a new chapter?

With the advent of the Adoption Support Fund (ASF) in England there is some long-overdue recognition that adopted children and their parents need and deserve support.

In response to concerns that too many adoptive families were being left to struggle alone, the Government introduced the ASF in May 2015, following a pilot year with several local authorities that showed that it had been helpful to adoptive families. The ASF is a pot of money, initially £19.3 million made available for one year, to pay for adoption support where this falls within the definition of "therapeutic intervention for the child". As of March 2016, the ASF had funded extra support for over 4,200 adoptive families.

The extra funding has been a welcome development, and although there are still questions about how the ASF is working in practice, in January 2016 the Government announced that funding for the ASF will continue, increasing year-on-year, for the next four years. In March 2016, the Government issued a policy paper containing some important changes to the ASF. These changes will come into force in April 2016, and include extending the eligibility criteria, including applying to children adopted from overseas, applying to all adopted young people up to the age of 21 and not 18 as previously, and has also been extended to cover Special Guardians who care for children who were previously looked after.

The ASF application process

In brief, adopters who have identified that they would like help for their child apply to the local authority that has responsibility for them for an assessment of their child's support needs. If the local authority's assessment indicates that therapeutic support for the child is needed, the local authority then applies to the ASF on behalf of the family. Once the application is approved by the ASF, the local authority is given the money to pay for the therapy identified in the assessment.

Which local authority should you apply to? For the first three years after the Adoption Order, the local authority that placed the child with you is responsible for assessing your adoption support needs. After three years it becomes the responsibility of the local authority where you live (if this is a different local authority).

The ASF applies to children who have been adopted from local authority care in England or adopted from Wales, Scotland or Northern Ireland but living in England and for whom the English local authority has the statutory responsibility to assess. It is also available for children adopted from overseas.

A placing local authority in England that has placed a child in Wales, Scotland or Northern Ireland can claim for services provided to the child there, for the first three years after the adoption.

You can apply for help for an adopted child up to and including the age of 21 (or 25 if the child has special needs with an Education and Health Care Plan).

Assessment

The process for undertaking an assessment is set out in regulations and they must be complied with. The regulations require that a written report is completed following the assessment process and that a copy of this report is sent to the adoptive family so that they can express their views on its accuracy and adequacy. If support services are being proposed as a result of the assessment, then these must be set out in that report. Following this consultation, the local authority then decides whether it will provide the services proposed and that includes making an application to the ASF. It should be noted that the regulations also require that somebody be identified who will monitor the effectiveness of the service provided, whether the timescales are being met, and what the outcomes are for the family.

An assessment is normally undertaken by a professional – usually a social worker – with specialist knowledge in adoption support. They should explore with the family the issues that have resulted in them requesting an assessment. How they do this will depend on the issues raised by the family, the history of these issues, the impact they are having and what to date has been tried in attempting to tackle the issues. In some cases, this may be relatively straightforward; in others, this may require a number of meetings in order to come to an agreed understanding about what has been happening, what is happening, and what to do about it. Other professionals, such as a psychologist, may need to be consulted where they have specialist knowledge. Above all, this assessment process should be carried out without undue delay and enable everybody to have his or her say and feel listened to, with an absence of any blame or fault finding.

Given what is known about children who are placed for adoption, any assessment must be open to the likelihood that the presenting problem may have a number of causes. For instance, learning difficulties may exist alongside heightened emotions and "strange" behaviour. This may be explained in a number of ways and it is important that the range of explanations is properly explored. Is there good evidence that this is an "attachment disorder", or may it be the emergence of an autistic spectrum disorder or possible foetal alcohol spectrum disorder? Sometimes it is very difficult to be clear and specific, sometimes it is easier. Both the assessing social worker and the family need to be open to these possibilities and where there are doubts, they may need to turn to specialists for help in understanding any of this in more detail. The ASF can be used to resource such specialist help. Turning to an intervention simply because it is recommended on the internet or by another parent may lead to following a false trail of help that may not help at all, or may make the situation worse.

These more complex issues raise the importance of considering a multidisciplinary approach. The child may need to be assessed by specialists from occupational therapy to speech and language therapy, educational and clinical psychologists and specialists in neuro-developmental trauma and attachment disorders. This may include making a referral to Child and Adolescent Mental Health Services (CAMHS).

What does a multidisciplinary assessment look like?

There are a number of adoption support agencies that undertake multidisciplinary assessments as well as Tier 3 and 4 CAMHS (see p24 for more information). The adoption agency Family Futures provides an integrated multidisciplinary approach to child assessment. Before undertaking any therapy, Family Futures recommends a comprehensive multidisciplinary assessment where the child and their family spend a day at the Family Futures Centre. Before this, a lot of information about the child and family is gathered from school, health reports and questionnaires completed by the child's parents to provide a detailed understanding of the child.

> Once this information has been gathered and analysed, the child and family spend the day at Family Futures where we provide therapeutic tasks for the family to engage with together. There will be time for parents to share their concerns and perceptions of their child's or children's difficulties. Each child is able to spend time with a therapist, who uses verbal and non-verbal creative art techniques to help them portray their beliefs, feelings, attachments and their inner world.

Further specialist assessments may be recommended or requested, including:

- A psychiatric assessment by a child and adolescent psychiatrist who can recommend a treatment programme;

- A sensory integration assessment by a paediatric occupational therapist who can recommend a remedial programme;

- A paediatric assessment by a consultant paediatrician, which may lead to a referral to appropriate NHS provision, if required;

- A cognitive assessment by a consultant psychologist to assess any areas of cognitive functioning difficulty and to advise on school and education.

www.familyfutures.co.uk

Adoptionplus is another agency that can provide a comprehensive and wide-ranging assessment of the therapeutic needs of the family.

> We use multiple methods of assessment and invite children and parents to take part in interviews, questionnaire methods and structured observation of interactions between them. This includes gaining an understanding of:
>
> - The presenting needs and strengths of the family;

- *The impact of the early experience of maltreatment on the child's attachment relationships, emotional regulation and emotional wellbeing;*

- *The impact of attachment experiences and behaviour on the capacity of parents to parent their children with confidence, empathy and joy.*

Adoptionplus also carries out neurodevelopmental assessments conducted by a consultant clinical psychologist and paediatric occupational therapist to clarify the effects of neglect and abuse on the child's development, including motor development, attention, planning, cognitive ability, learning, memory and sensory processing. They then liaise and feed back to people involved in the child's care, including schools, educational psychologists, GPs, paediatricians and mental health services.
www.adoptionplus.co.uk

NICE guidance on attachment for adopted children, children in care and those on the edge of care

The National Institute for Health and Care Excellence (NICE) has undertaken a comprehensive review of attachment, its assessment and treatment, reviewing all the evidence that is available from many years of research. The associated guidance makes a number of recommendations, taking into account:

- Personal factors, including the child's assessed attachment pattern and relationships;

- History of placements and placement changes;

- Child's educational experiences and attainment;

- Child's history of maltreatment or trauma;

- Child's physical health;

- Parental factors;

- Mental health problems and neuro-developmental conditions often associated with attachment difficulties, including antisocial behaviour and conduct disorders, attention deficit hyperactivity disorder (ADHD), autism, anxiety disorders (especially PTSD) and depression.

The guidance raises some significant questions about the link between the research evidence and current trends in practice. It is difficult to know what the longer-term impact will be of the guidance in moving practice towards a stronger evidence base. But for adoptive families, there should always be a question in engaging with any profession or service that addresses the following: 'Does the evidence suggest that you or we are asking the right questions and coming up with the right answers?' Openness, curiosity and the ability to explore issues from different perspectives are marks of maturity and wisdom. A simple conviction that there is only one way to solve a problem and 'I know that I am right' is not a helpful way to address some of the complex problems adoptive families are faced with.

After the assessment

As noted above, the regulations require that the social worker or other professional who carried out the assessment discuss it with you to ensure that it is accurate, balanced and based on all the evidence collected in the course of the assessment. It must also identify what services are being proposed and, where these are therapeutic services for your child, whether the local authority will apply for funding from the ASF. Your post-adoption social worker will advise on what he or she thinks would best meet your family's needs, on the basis of their assessment, but of course you can also do your own research. You should have some input into this, including the choice of provider and their location. It may be that you have identified a specific practitioner and you should discuss this as a part of the assessment. This includes being able to go to whichever provider best suits your needs and not being limited by your local authority's borders.

When the local authority has reviewed the assessment and decided to provide services, and if these include therapeutic services for the child, then the local authority will inform you that this is their plan and set out the detail of what this involves. This may include an application to the ASF with a costing for everything that is being requested. For example, it may make an application for 20 sessions of Theraplay.

Within five working days the ASF makes its decision, and funds are distributed to local authorities at the end of every month.

What is covered by the ASF – and what's not covered?

As has been identified already, the ASF is primarily focused on therapeutic services for your child.

The following information comes from the First4Adoption website:

What support will I receive through the ASF?

The Fund will provide money for a range of therapeutic services that are identified to help achieve the following positive outcomes for you and your child:

- Improved relationships with friends, family members, teachers and school staff

- Improved engagement with learning

- Improved emotional regulation and behaviour management

- Improved confidence and ability to enjoy a positive family life and social relationships

To achieve these outcomes the Fund will pay for therapeutic support and services including but not restricted to:

- Therapeutic parenting training

- Complex assessments (e.g. CAMHS assessment, multidisciplinary assessment including education and health, cognitive and neuropsychological assessment, other mental health needs assessment)

- Dyadic Developmental Psychotherapy

- Theraplay

- Filial therapy

- Creative therapies e.g. art, music, drama, play

- Eye Movement Desensitisation and Reprocessing Therapy (EMDR)

- Non-Violent Resistance (NVR)

- Sensory integration therapy/Sensory attachment therapy

- Multi Systemic Therapy

- Psychotherapy

- Specialist clinical assessments where required (e.g. Foetal Alcohol Spectrum Disorder)

- Extensive life story work with a therapeutic intervention (where therapy is used to help the young person understand and cope with the trauma and difficulties that their life story work might revisit)

- Short breaks/respite care (where it is part of a therapeutic intervention)

What will the ASF not cover?

There are regulations that identify a range of adoption support services that the local authority must provide as a part of its adoption support service (see pp26–7). The services that must be provided include groups that enable those affected by adoption to discuss their experiences and concerns, arrangements to facilitate contact, and services to help where there is a disruption to the placement. The availability of these services depends on the status of the person for whom they are being considered with differences depending on whether a child has been adopted from care, or has been adopted from overseas or by a step-parent. There are also differences depending on whether the people needing support are the adoptive parents of these children or the birth parents. The responsibility for all of these services rests with the local authority, is financed by them, and overseen by an Adoption Support Services Adviser.

It is important to note that the ASF only pays for services that are defined as "therapeutic services for the child". While the other services must be available, they are not covered by the ASF. Local authorities continue to be responsible for all the other identified statutory support services they are required to provide (see p26, *What other adoption support is available?*). But they may be able to argue the case for ASF funding if, for example, a young person needs mediation with birth parents in preparation for re-establishing contact or if a child needs more intensive life story work, for example, because he is having difficulty in dealing with anger about his birth relatives or is struggling with painful experiences from his past.

First4Adoption explains that:

The ASF will also not pay for:
- Support for physical medical conditions

- Speech and language therapy, physical therapy, occupational therapy, and other universal health services

- Education support

- Membership of clubs and organisations

- Legal support

- Support provided by private sector and third sector organisations that are not Ofsted registered unless commissioned through local authorities

- Training of staff

- Support not delivered in England, Scotland, Wales and Northern Ireland

- Animal, pet or equine therapy[1]

- Ex-local authority (associate) social workers

One local authority commented that, with the help of the ASF, it is now able to provide more support, sooner. For example, it can provide support to teenage adopted children whereas before, it could not have put in support until the tensions reached crisis point.

The ASF may also be used to pay for travel expenses if, for example, a parent needs to take the child to therapy a long way away.

Who provides therapeutic services?

Some adoption agencies (both local authority and voluntary adoption agencies) already provide certain therapies and parenting courses to their adopters as part of their existing adoption support programme.

Eligible providers of services under the ASF include local authorities, independent providers and Child and Adolescent Mental Health Services (see below). Therapy from CAMHS should be available on the NHS but some NHS providers may also offer services that are commissioned by the local authority and paid for by the ASF. The ASF can potentially pay for adoption support services where an agency needs to buy them in, for example, from another adoption support agency or an independent provider.

All providers of adoption support services have to be registered and inspected by Ofsted and meet the relevant national minimum standards. Apart from NHS services, only Ofsted-regulated providers can provide adoption support. The list of providers includes local authorities, organisations like PAC-UK, After

---

1 Equine therapy is currently not funded by the ASF; this is due to be reviewed.

Adoption, Family Futures and Coram as well as many much smaller organisations. Independent providers may be working in private practice and be Ofsted-registered in their own right or they may be commissioned by a local authority to provide services, in which case they are covered by the local authority's Ofsted registration.

When can you apply?

From the point of the placement of your child, you will have an adoption support plan. This is likely to cover a wide range of issues – practical, financial, parenting support, and visits from various professionals. An application to the ASF can be made as soon as the child is placed with you. The ASF can now be used to provide therapeutic support to children from the point at which they are placed with their adoptive families, rather than from the point of the Adoption Order. You can request an assessment at any time up to your child's 19th birthday (25 if your child has an education, health and care plan).

If your circumstances change after you have had an assessment, you can request another assessment. You can also reapply to the ASF after the support has ended, if you still need support and if you and the local authority feel that this would be of benefit.

Teething problems?

Some adopters are finding that they are still facing long delays waiting for local authorities to carry out the assessment or make the application. There is some variation in how different local authorities are using the ASF – some have prioritised their procedures in order to reduce any delay, others have yet to do this in a way that adopters need. And there are concerns that in some parts of the country, therapies are still difficult to access because there are few therapists working there compared with, for example, London and other big cities.

Al Coates, Sally Donovan and Jenny Jones are adoptive parents who also write and campaign about adoption issues. When the ASF had been operating for a few months, they were given the opportunity to gather adoptive parents' experiences of accessing the ASF and feed them back to the Department for Education's Expert Advisory Group.

Al Coates wrote in his blog *ASF Update: Adopters' Experiences* about what they had found out:

1

Even though the fund is still in its infancy there are many positive experiences and we did our best to reflect them...A significant number of adopters have come to us and shared their challenges and difficulties. Clear themes have come through:

- *Social workers having no, limited or incorrect information in relation to the scope and process of the ASF*

- *Families waiting unacceptable lengths of time for assessment or even contact with social workers*

- *Where there have been acrimonious or difficult relationships between families and Adoption Services they remain a barrier to accessing the ASF*

- *Families that adopted through voluntary adoption agencies struggling to access services through their local authority*

- *Adoptees with very complex needs or large sibling groups that have multiple needs*

- *Adopters being told that they need to have the assessment of need completed by CAMHS, in some cases where there is no provision or where relationships are challenging.*

Coates said that he sees a genuine drive in the Department for Education to see the ASF used in the most productive manner and accessed by as many families as possible:

In some respects we are trying to change cultures and practice within local authorities that the DfE has limited control over on a case by case level. Pressure can be, and has been, brought to bear but that's like us fixing a puncture while riding the bike, not easy.

For more on the ASF and how it works, see www.adoptionsupportfund.co.uk and www.first4adoption.org.uk.

Child and Adolescent Mental Health Services (CAMHS)

Child and Adolescent Mental Health Services (CAMHS) are part of the NHS and provide specialist mental health services for children and young people across the UK. There are four different levels, or tiers, of CAMHS services (though not every area will have each tier represented in its services).

- At Tier 1, practitioners are not mental health specialists – they include GPs, health visitors, school nurses, teachers and social workers.

- At Tier 2, practitioners have specialist skills and knowledge in child and adolescent mental health – such as mental health workers, counsellors and psychologists. They work in community and primary care settings such as health centres.

- At Tier 3, there is usually a multidisciplinary team or service in a community mental health clinic or child psychiatry outpatient service, providing a specialised service for children and young people with more complex and persistent disorders. The team is likely to include child and adolescent psychiatrists, clinical psychologists, child psychotherapists, community psychiatric nurses and arts, music and drama therapists.

- Tier 4 services are for children and young people with the most severe problems. They are based in day units, highly specialised outpatient units and hospital inpatient units, and have specialist teams (for example, for children with eating disorders and children who have been sexually abused). They usually serve a much wider area, from which children with serious mental health problems can be referred by the lower tier services.

Most practitioners working in Tiers 3 and 4 will be working for NHS trusts (e.g. mental health trusts). Services are commissioned locally through Clinical Commissioning Groups[1] rather than by the local authority or primary care trust.

You can ask your GP, your child's school or an adoption support worker to refer your child to CAMHS.

What happens at CAMHS?

First, your child will have an assessment in which the clinic professionals will explore the issues that concern you. They may see you together as a family, your child by him or herself, or in other combinations depending on what needs to be explored with whom. The assessment may include completing questionnaires or other tests as well as discussions. You should be told about the purpose of any

---

1   For local information visit www.nhs.uk/Service-Search/Clinical%20Commissioning%20 Group/LocationSearch/1

test and it is very important that you have an opportunity to fully present the issues, ask questions and discuss what is being proposed and might happen. After the assessment you will be told of the outcome of the assessment and, possibly, given a diagnosis. If the CAMHS service you have seen cannot offer support itself then they should refer you on to another service, perhaps a higher tier service or another NHS service.

The kind of help CAMHS may be able to give depends on your child's needs and whether they have the appropriate practitioner with the right level of skill within their service. It is important to remember the wide range of issues that CAMHS deals with, including neuro-developmental disorders such as autistic spectrum disorders, emotional difficulties such as severe depression and/or anxiety, and the beginning of a serious mental health difficulty such as psychosis. The underlying causation of these many issues can be a combination of genetic factors as well as adverse experiences from exposure to drugs and alcohol before birth, malnourishment prior to or after birth and poor parenting or care including abuse and/or neglect. And rather than there being a single cause, there are probably a number of causative factors. There will always be an element of uncertainty in any diagnosis. The professionals will explain this to you and explain how they will take this into account when offering help for your child.

CAMHS will draw on a range of interventions that are known to be effective. For many of the more common diagnoses, they will follow the recommendations of the National Institute for Health and Care Excellence.[1] These may be supplemented by particular local experience and expertise. Again, there should be a full explanation of the reasons behind any suggested intervention and what it means in practice.

Current concerns about CAMHS

CAMHS and adoption support services should work closely together but unfortunately there are many reports of cases where this is not happening. Many adopters who try the CAMHS route for their child to be seen find that there are long waiting lists. And while some CAMHS services do have psychologists and other staff with a good understanding of adoption-related issues, many don't.

The issues were highlighted in a 2015 report from the Government's Children and Young People's Mental Health Taskforce (2015):

> *...GPs, schools and other professionals such as social workers and youth workers often feel as frustrated as the children and their parents. They*

---

1   www.nice.org.uk/guidance

want to do the right thing, but have not necessarily been equipped to play their part or been provided with clear access routes to expertise and for referring to targeted and specialist support. Professionals working in child and adolescent mental health services are equally aware of the challenges that come from balancing identified need with available resource. (p35)

The report makes a number of proposals and the Government has announced a plan of action, including an investment of further resources to improve CAMHS services by 2020. On the subject of trauma-focused care, the report says:

Many mental health service users of all ages have problems directly attributable to severe neglect and/or trauma in the early years...

Enhanced training for staff working with children and young people would lead to greater professional awareness of the impact of trauma, abuse or neglect on mental health. This should be coupled with effective treatment, including:

...Those children and young people who have been sexually abused and/or exploited should receive a comprehensive specialist initial assessment and referral to appropriate services providing evidence-based interventions according to their need. There will be a smaller group who are suffering from a mental health disorder, who would benefit from referral to a specialist mental health service. (p52)

The announcement recognises the importance and urgency of improving CAMHS and has been welcomed. Alongside the Adoption Support Fund, this is an important development.

What other adoption support is available?

In 2013, the Department for Education issued what it called an "Adoption Passport", a list of the entitlements of adoptive families in England, including:

- Priority access for their child to the school parents think best meets the child's needs

- The Pupil Premium (£1,900 per year in 2015), which is given to state schools for each child adopted from care to support their wellbeing and attainment in school

- A free early education place for children of two or older, for 570 hours a year

- The right to adoption pay and leave
- Priority for council housing

According to the Adoption Passport, adoption support services provided and funded by local authorities for children adopted from care may (depending on circumstances) include:

- Counselling, information and advice
- Help with behavioural, attachment and other problems
- Money, e.g. to help with special care needs, or for former foster carers
- Help with contact between an adopted child and his or her birth family
- Meetings and events to enable groups of adopters and adopted children to get together
- Training to help adopters to meet the needs of their adopted child
- Short breaks for an adopted child with another carer
- Help where an adoption breaks down
- An Adoption Support Services Adviser to help adopters access adoption support and other specialist services, such as Child and Adolescent Mental Health Services (CAMHS). The Adoption Support Services Adviser's details should be available on the local authority's website.

Support in school

The Pupil Premium provides funding to help school staff give extra support to certain pupils. These include disadvantaged children and children of families in the armed forces as well as looked after children and adopted children. It applies to all adopted children (those who were adopted from care, not from overseas) from reception through to year 11.

Schools are meant to invest the extra resources in specific support measures to address issues that may be preventing children from reaching their potential. There is some flexibility in how they use the Pupil Premium funding – for example, they could provide one-to-one tuition or training for staff in attachment issues. The money does not have to be spent directly on the individual child but schools should certainly be able to explain to you how your child has benefited from the way the school has used it.

As well as priority access to your chosen school and the Pupil Premium, there are other kinds of support with education that can be invaluable for adoptive parents.

Virtual Schools and Virtual School Heads are a way of keeping tabs on the educational progress of looked after children and improving their educational outcomes by monitoring their progress and identifying and suggesting solutions where problems arise. Many looked after children fall behind at school because of their difficult early experiences, long or frequent absences, changes of school, or behaviour problems. In the education White Paper published in March 2016 (*Education Excellence Everywhere*), the Government confirms that it would look at extending the current role of the Virtual School Heads and the role and responsibilities of the school designated teacher for looked after children to also support children who have left care under an Adoption Order.

Gareth Marr is an adoptive father who has made it his personal crusade to raise awareness in schools and with teachers of the difficulties faced by adopted children and the solutions that can help. Adopted children, after all, are likely to have been looked after children until the point at which they were adopted. Their educational difficulties do not simply disappear overnight. He writes about these issues, gives talks at schools and to local authority children's services, trains teachers, and lobbies the Department for Education.

As a result of his approach to Alison Alexander, the Director of Children's Services in his own local authority (LA), Windsor & Maidenhead, Virtual School support is now offered to all adopted children in the borough throughout their education, no matter which local authority placed the child. In June 2015, Marr and Alexander invited all LAs in England to a seminar to make the case for all LAs to implement the same policy.

Here are just a few of the points from Gareth Marr's blog, in which he argues that all adopted children should have the support of a Virtual School.

Why adopted children need and deserve the support of Virtual Schools

- Adoptive parents are not specialists in education practice and in most cases will not have developed the understanding and support network that comes from bringing up a child from birth – meeting other families, getting to know how infant and primary schools work. They have a child placed with them with possibly one day's training on trauma and attachment and then are left to sort out that child's educational needs without any expert support. Virtual School Heads have all the expertise and the knowledge of the local schools to provide the support needed in finding the right school and helping the child and parent start their new school life well. This support can be needed years after placement. An infant can be four years old before starting school. Help is really important at KS2/KS3 transition (primary to secondary school).

- It is generally accepted that transitions are the main triggers for trauma-related problems arising. After the major transition to an adoptive family, usually from foster care, the next transition is "going to school". And school transitions then take place through the rest of childhood and adolescence. Hourly, daily, weekly, termly, yearly, at Key Stages, the child experiences change. Every one of these transitions can create anxiety for the child, which may manifest themselves in behavioural problems, connecting with past experiences of loss, anxiety or trauma. A looked after child will have the support of a Virtual School Head, a designated teacher, a personal education plan, and trained school staff to help manage these transitions. An adopted child has none of this but needs the same help. Their parents may struggle to provide it. A traumatised adopted child can be in the same class as a looked after child. One gets support, the other doesn't. This is wrong.

- The Adoption Social social media site surveyed 110 parents and 181 children during Autistic Spectrum Disorder (ASD) Awareness Week in 2015. These were the results:

  - *27% of children have ASD compared to 1.1% of the general population*

  - *15% of families had at least one child with an ASD diagnosis*

  - *Not one child had an ASD diagnosis at the time of placement*

  - *70% of families reported other medical/mental health conditions diagnosed post-Adoption Order.*

- All of these children will need varying levels of support in school yet none was diagnosed at placement. Another reason why Virtual School support is needed for all adopted children. One cannot predict when issues will arise. Virtual School support could transform these children's life expectations and help their families have the happy life they dreamt about when adopting.

- There are many mixed reports of schools' practice with Pupil Premium Plus. Whilst some are doing a really good job, working with parents and helping children, others are refusing to talk to parents and spending the funds without any recognition of the child's needs. A VSH is ideally placed to work with the school to ensure effective use of the PPP and measure the success of the spending and interventions.

Extracts from *Support for Adopted Children at School – the biggest campaign day yet!* Blog post by Gareth Marr, June 28, 2015 (http://lushlife7.com/author/garethmarr7/)

Marr also stresses the importance of schools and teachers being "attachment-aware" so that they respond appropriately to adopted children's trauma-related difficulties and behaviours. More and more schools are becoming "attachment-aware" thanks to the work of people like Marr and Louise Bomber, a well-known therapist and author who trains teachers and other school staff to support pupils with attachment difficulties in schools.[1]

Learning from the prototype ASF

In December 2015, the final report from the analysis of the prototype Adoption Support Fund (ASF), undertaken for the Department for Education by the Colebrook Centre for Evidence and Implementation, with Adoption UK, was published. It draws on a programme of work that reviewed the implementation of the prototype version of the ASF and early evidence of its impact and potential. The prototype ASF was tested in ten local authorities and the prototype period, June 2014 to May 2015, was used to refine key features and operating procedures of the ASF. The report is available at www.gov.uk/government/uploads/system/uploads/attachment_data/file/489538/DFE-RR467__Adoption_Support_Fund_learning_from_the_prototype__research_report.pdf and contains an analysis of the use of the prototype ASF, the experience of families using services funded by the ASF, key aspects of implementation in local authority adoption support services, early evidence of the impact of the prototype ASF on local adoption support systems and key messages. It also looks at early outcomes from therapeutic interventions.

---

1   For a helpful booklet, see www.celcis.org/knowledge-bank/search-bank/looked-after-and-learning

SECTION 2
About therapy

What is therapy?

"Therapy" comes from the Greek word "therapeia", which means "curing" or "healing".

Therapies can take many forms, such as medication (drug treatment), physiotherapy or speech therapy. **Psychotherapy** – which comes in a wide range of different types and methods – is "talking treatment" for emotional distress and mental health problems.

Of course, throughout human history people have always helped each other through mental and emotional distress by listening and talking with each other about their feelings. But the first specific approach to using talking and listening as a therapy was psychoanalysis, developed by Sigmund Freud at the beginning of the 20th century. In his Vienna consulting room, he explored his patients' thoughts, dreams, fantasies and childhood experiences to try and work out what was going on in their unconscious minds that was making them ill.

Today there are many different types of psychotherapy. Some, like psychoanalysis, look at the impact of past experiences while others focus more on people's current problems and behaviour. But they all use some kind of communication between the therapist and the client as the basis for bringing about change. In a series of structured meetings, the therapist creates a safe space in which the person (child or adult) can use verbal or non-verbal ways of communicating their feelings, their fears and anxieties.

So many therapies…

Hundreds of different therapies have come into being since Freud first developed the theory and practice of psychoanalysis; some have fallen by the wayside while others have become more popular. Different therapies are based on different theories or models of how people become the way they are, and how and why they change or stay the same. So each therapy has its own particular understanding of human development, personality and behaviour, which therapists use as the basis for offering treatment.

Psychodynamic therapy is based on the teachings of Freud. Like psychoanalysis, this is an approach that looks at the causes of emotional difficulties, which often lie in early childhood – it is a way of bringing people's unconscious feelings to the surface so that they can experience them, understand them and resolve them.

In the 1920s **behaviour therapy** came into vogue – this focused on modifying the way that people behaved and helping them develop more positive habits, rather than delving into their unconscious mind or looking at their past experiences. It was based on the idea of "conditioning": certain behaviours are rewarded by some form of positive consequence that reinforces the behaviour, making it more likely that we will exhibit that behaviour again, while other behaviours that are not rewarded or have a negative consequence will become less common.

A later variation, emerging in the 1970s, is **cognitive behaviour therapy**, which combines cognitive psychology – with its emphasis on thought processes, irrational beliefs and dysfunctional attitudes – with behaviour therapy. This is widely used today – including within the NHS – as a treatment for depression and anxiety, among other conditions. Cognitive behaviour therapy is based on the idea that our thoughts and beliefs determine our behaviour and that by bringing about more positive ways of thinking, we can break harmful habits and behaviour patterns.

Recent years have seen what's been called a **"third wave of behaviour therapy"**, which combines cognitive behaviour therapy with ideas of mindfulness and acceptance.

Expressive arts or creative therapies use drawing, painting, clay modelling, drama and music as the basis for communicating and developing a relationship between the therapist and the client. **Play therapy** is often used with young children. The aim is to help them to explore and process their feelings and anxieties when they may be too young or not able to do this in words alone.

Why are there so many different therapies?

You might think that rather than having so many different therapies on offer, it would be simpler just to find out which one works best and offer that one. But of course it's not as simple as that. There are many schools of thought, as we have seen, so therapists offer the particular therapy or combination of therapies that they feel has the most to offer.

Individual clients may have a preference for a particular type of therapy, or respond better to a particular type. Some therapies may be suitable for use with slight or mild problems, while more complex or severe problems may require a different approach. Some therapies can be used with very young children who haven't yet learned to speak, while others rely on talking. Some therapies focus on the client's individual problems, while others – **systemic therapies** – look at how the client functions in relation to other people.

And often there is a degree of overlap between the various approaches. Some therapists specialise in one particular approach; others don't believe that only one approach works with everyone and prefer to use several models or theories together depending on the person's problems. **Integrative psychotherapy** is one of the most recent schools of thought in psychotherapy – it brings together elements of various different therapies and tailors the treatment to each individual.

All therapies aim to bring about the same kinds of result – they just go about it by different routes.

Whatever the type of therapy, the trusting and supportive relationship that develops between the therapist and the client is vital.

Therapies as part of post-adoption support

Some psychological therapies used as part of post-adoption support are general therapies – such as psychotherapy, cognitive behaviour therapy, expressive arts therapies and sensory integration therapy – for children (adopted or not) who have a range of mental health conditions such as post-traumatic stress disorder, anxiety, depression, self-harm and eating disorders.

Others have been developed for use with looked after and adopted children who have experienced neglect, abuse and developmental trauma. In recent years, there has been an ever-increasing focus on the neuroscience of attachment and developmental trauma and how these experiences impact on children's brain development and functioning. This is the theory that experiencing neglect or abuse in early life can lead to the brain being "wired differently" and that children who have experienced hurt and fear and rejection perceive the world, and relationships, differently from those who haven't.

This increasing body of research on the neuroscience of attachment and trauma has informed the work of renowned American clinicians such as Dr Bruce Perry (see pp68–9) and Dan Hughes (see p56) as well as experts in the

UK with international reputations, such as Dr Margot Sunderland and Kate Cairns. They have taken the findings and used them to develop parenting approaches and training for parents, carers and practitioners to help reduce children's anxiety and regulate their emotions. Secondary trauma (for those living or working with traumatised children) and the need for self-care and self-regulation for parents and carers are an important part of this.

Some trauma-focused and attachment-focused therapies involve the therapist working together with the adoptive parents and their child, helping to build attachment and empathy. For example, various forms of therapy involving the child and the parents include filial therapy, Theraplay and Dyadic Developmental Psychotherapy (these and other therapies are described in Section 3). Training aims to help adoptive parents to understand the reasons why their child behaves as he or she does and provide day-to-day parenting strategies to help the child function better.

Family therapy looks at the whole family, and the relationships within it, rather than simply focusing on the child and his or her problems. Systemic therapies look at relationships with other people both inside and outside the family. The idea is that the child should not be treated in isolation but helped to understand and solve his or her problems in relation to the important people in his or her life, and the therapist also looks at how other people can offer support.

A particular therapy may be used alone or, often, in combination with other forms of therapy. Sometimes a therapy is used in combination with medication, for example, in attention deficit hyperactivity disorder (ADHD). Medication is not, however, recommended for attachment difficulties.

There are also courses for adoptive parents in dealing with specific problems, such as aggression and violence from their child directed towards them. There is more information about these programmes in the following section. Some of these therapies and programmes can be provided under the Adoption Support Fund in England (see p13).

Do therapies work?

It's a simple question, but unfortunately, it's impossible to give a simple answer. In any case, therapy doesn't usually aim or claim to offer a "cure":

What it actually aims to do is to provide you with an opportunity to work through your problems and equip you with understanding, coping skills and tools to allow a healthier state of mind and to improve your psychological wellbeing.

AdEPT project, University of Sheffield Centre for Psychological Services Research (www.supportingsafetherapy.org)

The aim of therapy in the context of post-adoption support is to help adopted children and young people deal with the legacy of early experiences of trauma, neglect and abuse, loss, grief, identity issues, emotional and behavioural problems and other difficulties directly or indirectly resulting from their early experiences or their adoption.

So, if therapies don't provide a cure, are they at least effective in bringing about some improvement?

Caveats and controversies

With so many different therapies and other interventions – many of them claiming to be effective – it would be great to be able to say that 'Therapies A, B and C have been shown to work well, while therapies D, E and F don't work.' Some people who have tried a particular therapy, or whose child has had a particular therapy, and found it helpful may well recommend it to others. And therapy organisations and individual therapists often publish case studies that show how they have helped a particular client.

Some people prefer to be guided by research outcomes rather than personal opinions. While personal opinions and experiences may be valid and some therapeutic approaches can sound as though they make good sense, they don't provide the kind of robust evidence that the scientific community likes to see (see box overleaf). The problem is that this kind of evidence is often lacking in the case of therapies for post-adoption support.

"Proving" that a particular therapy is effective requires that it is evaluated by means of a rigorously conducted scientific trial. Some conditions and problems improve or resolve by themselves over time in any case, with or without therapy, so it's important to establish whether any improvement was due to the therapy or would have happened in any case. And it's well known that simply having extra attention and believing that the therapy is going to help (the "placebo effect") can in itself bring about an improvement, regardless of the therapy.

Research trials involve, for example, giving the therapy to a sufficiently large group of people, and comparing their results with a group of people with a similar condition at a similar level of severity who did not have the therapy. Or it could involve measuring the severity of the condition in a group of people, then applying the treatment or intervention for a limited time, and then measuring again.

Trials have to be conducted properly in order to show if the therapy is having a genuine effect. The people in the control group and the group who have the actual therapy must be randomly allocated to the groups. The levels of improvement in the two groups after the course of treatment (and sometimes for a long follow-up period) are compared. There are statistical tests to compare the levels of improvement in the "experimental" and "control" groups to find out if any difference between them is actually statistically significant and not just down to chance.

So this is where things get difficult. There is research evidence for the effectiveness of certain types of therapy such as child and adolescent psychotherapy and cognitive behaviour therapy as well as training and support for adoptive parents. But there are a number of other therapies – some of which are widely used in adoption support and highly regarded by many people – which have quite simply not been properly evaluated. (And they have been included in the list of those qualifying for funding from the Adoption Support Fund even though there is no robust evidence to support them yet.)

Sometimes this is because the therapies are relatively new and these kinds of clinical trials have simply not been done. The entire field of therapy for mental health has not been around all that long – it's generally considered as starting in around 1900 with Freud. Therapy with children is not yet 100 years old. Several of the therapies used as part of post-adoption support and discussed in this book are very recent developments, so building up what's called an "evidence base" for them is a work in progress in many cases.

Sometimes studies have been carried out and are quoted extensively by the people offering the therapy, but if you dig a little deeper you find that the trials have shortcomings and therefore the validity of the "evidence" presented is actually questioned by other experts. And without a proper evidence base, you can't say for sure that a particular therapy works.

2

Unfortunately, it's beyond the scope of this book to evaluate the validity of the claims made for the effectiveness of all the different therapies that are outlined in Section 3. But when you are looking into claims made for therapies, it's important to bear in mind what's been called the "Woozle effect". This is named after a Winnie the Pooh story by A A Milne, in which Winnie the Pooh and Piglet start to follow some tracks in the snow. They believe they are following a "Woozle". As they continue to follow the tracks, the tracks multiply. Christopher Robin eventually explains to them that they have actually been following their own prints in the snow while going round and round a tree. It's an analogy for what can happen when researchers quote in their own work the results of trials that have been done in the past. A particular trial can end up being quoted so many times in the scientific literature that, even though the original trial may actually have been of very poor quality, everyone assumes that the findings were valid and the therapy must have been shown to be effective.

But even where well-conducted trials have shown some evidence of effectiveness for a particular therapy, it does not mean that any *individual* will definitely benefit. The therapy might work for one child but not for another, and it's impossible to understand why. There are always individual differences between people that mean it's hard to predict how someone will respond to a particular therapy.

And there is some evidence that, regardless of the type of therapy, a positive outcome depends on the **quality of the therapeutic relationship** that develops between the therapist and the adult, child or young person who is undergoing the therapy.

Reviewing the evidence

In the UK, an organisation called NICE (National Institute for Health and Care Excellence) assesses the available evidence around certain treatments – anything from drugs to surgery to psychotherapy. NICE approves certain treatments to be made available on the NHS but it rejects others. Its aim is to ensure that treatments and therapies that are offered are genuinely effective and represent the best use of public funds.

NICE has recently published a report on the treatment of attachment disorders in children. It recommended parenting training programmes – in particular, one called VIPP-SD (see Section 3) but said little about other forms of therapy that are currently being used or that are available under the Adoption Support Fund in England.

Recognising that there is little hard evidence in this area, it states (2015, p29):

> *In the absence of trial data, if non-evidence-based interventions are to be chosen, it would seem sensible to choose therapies that are based in empirically supported theory of how secure attachments develop, and on established psychological therapies which address related issues such as self-esteem, emotional regulation, enhancing communication and family functioning, as well as psycho-educational interventions that help to explain the impact of maltreatment and the nature of attachment relationships to parents/carers either individually, or in groups. Much of the work is dyadic – working with the parent and child together – which makes sense given the nature of attachment relationships and the challenges of building a trusting relationship with a therapist.*
>
> *Work that relates to reducing shame, experiencing empathy, learning to co-regulate emotional and physiological arousal is a promising area for this dyadic and family work.*

In 2016, a draft report was commissioned by the DfE, which aims to review the evidence for a range of therapies. This report, *The Independent Evidence Review of Post-Adoption Support Interventions*, has been written by Laura Stock, Dr Thomas Spielhoer and Matthew Gieve from the Tavistock Institute of Human Relations.

The report looks at 15 therapies covered by the Adoption Support Fund. It aims to improve understanding of the origins of the therapies; how they are delivered; what they seek to achieve; what evidence on their effectiveness currently exists; and what further research could be undertaken to improve this evidence base.

This is an initial step in a longer-term process led by the DfE to improve the evidence base in post-adoption therapeutic support, and to explore the effectiveness of these approaches in achieving successful outcomes for adopted children and their families.

SECTION 3
Therapies and therapeutic parenting support

Some of the therapies included here can be used to address problems stemming from attachment disorder and developmental trauma as well as being useful with conditions such as foetal alcohol spectrum disorders. We have also covered therapeutic parenting programmes, which are usually delivered to groups of adoptive parents, and treatment programmes designed to support parents in managing serious behaviour problems and child-to-parent violence.

CHILD PSYCHOTHERAPY

Core principles

Child psychotherapists explore the causes of distress and problematic behaviour by focusing on early life experiences and relationships and the ways in which these become embedded in the emotional life of the individual child. The relationship between the therapist and the child is key to the effectiveness of bringing about therapeutic change. Providing a safe space and a trusting relationship between the therapist and the child within which the child can explore their fears, anger, distress and other feelings, will directly enable them to make sense of why they feel and behave the way they do. In turn they will be more able to manage difficult emotions without turning to damaging and destructive ways of expressing them.

Child psychotherapy can be used with a wide range of difficulties, including depression, anxiety, behaviour and eating disorders, learning difficulties and disabilities, developmental issues and personality disorders, as well as the consequences of abuse and neglect.

History

During the 1920s, the psychoanalysts Melanie Klein and Anna Freud (the youngest child of Sigmund Freud, founder of psychoanalysis) began to explore, from their own perspectives, how Freud's discoveries with adult patients could be extended to help troubled children. At the same time, the "child guidance" movement was being established in the UK. In 1938 Freud came to England with her father to escape the Nazis. He died in 1939. Anna Freud set up a centre for young war victims and, later, an orphanage and continued her work and research in London.

The Association of Child Psychotherapists was founded in 1949, establishing child psychotherapy as a new profession with its own professional body, training council and rules. In the late 1940s, training courses for child psychotherapists were set up in London by Dr John Bowlby at the Tavistock Clinic and by Anna Freud at the Hampstead Clinic (later to become the Anna Freud Centre). Other training courses followed in various locations in the second half of the 20th century, and in 2003, the Northern School of Child and Adolescent Psychotherapy was established by the NHS to address the shortage of child and adolescent psychotherapists in the north of England.

In the mid-1990s, child and adolescent psychotherapists were recognised as core members of Child and Adolescent Mental Health Services (CAMHS) within the NHS.

The Association of Child Psychotherapists is the regulatory body for the profession. It has over 900 members working in the UK and abroad.

What the therapy involves

Psychotherapy is a "talking treatment" and the therapist will tailor the approach to the individual child. With young children the therapist will look at what they are communicating through their behaviour and through play or drawing. Older children and teenagers are more likely to be able to express what they feel in words.

Originating from an early, dominant psychoanalytic perspective, there are now many variations of child psychotherapy, which have a different focus or different methods – some, like psychodynamic therapy, for example, focus on unconscious thought processes that manifest themselves in behaviour. The therapist helps and encourages the child to explore troubling thoughts and feelings and to work through them.

Another example is cognitive behaviour therapy, in which the therapist looks at the "here and now" of the person's behaviour and helps them to change the thought processes that are causing their behaviour problems, depression, anxiety, and so on.

In some other models, the psychotherapist may see the parents with or without their child, to explore what is happening at home and help them make sense of the child's behaviour. Sometimes the therapy sessions involve the whole family (family therapy).

Below, we look at some specific types of psychotherapy that are often used with adopted children and families.

The sessions

A psychotherapist is likely to see your child for weekly sessions lasting up to an hour. The duration of psychotherapy can be from just a few sessions to several years.

Child psychotherapists are core professionals within CAMHS, which is part of the NHS, as well as working in hospitals, children's centres and private family therapy centres and post-adoption services, such as Family Futures, or in private practice. They often work as part of a multidisciplinary team and often see children and young people who have severe difficulties or where other therapies have not produced the desired effect.

CREATIVE ARTS THERAPIES AND PLAY THERAPY

Also known as "expressive arts therapies", this group of therapies includes creative therapies like art, music, drama, storytelling and play therapy.

Core principles

Sometimes it is hard for children to put their feelings into words. They may become withdrawn or "act out" their difficult emotions by being aggressive. Creative therapies use music, art, drama, storytelling and play as a way of reaching children, engaging with them and giving them a way to communicate and express themselves when they find talking difficult or when they are still too young to be able to verbalise their thoughts and feelings.

An essential element is developing a relationship between the child or young person and the therapist, whether that is built through, for example, painting, making clay figures, making music together or games and play. The relationship develops over a series of regular sessions.

'The child's natural musicality motivates them to listen and participate, and often enables them to concentrate for longer than usual,' says the British Association for Music Therapy in its factsheet, *Music Therapy in the Early Years*. Children learn to take turns, anticipate, listen, concentrate and respond. Making music with another person (the therapist or perhaps a parent) encourages the child's awareness of him or herself and others.

Because children are doing something they enjoy, this encourages them to engage with the therapist and to look forward to the sessions. Whether they are drawing, making a clay model or making music, the therapist can respond sensitively to what the child has produced, giving him or her a sense of being "heard".

The US art therapy pioneer Margaret Naumburg said free art expression 'becomes a form of symbolic speech which...leads to an increase in verbalisation in the course of therapy'.

Stories and drama can also be used in therapy to provide the opportunity for a child or adult to explore what has happened to them and what they hope for, by reviewing and enacting scenes from their past, present and future.

The British Association for Dramatherapists says:

> *Because emotions in real life can become overwhelming, we sometimes block them out or retreat from them. In a fictional reality, we can allow ourselves to feel things without having to deny their presence because we know fiction protects us but also allows us to be involved. The fiction can filter powerful feelings through to us but they do not engulf us, allowing us to acknowledge them and unlock some of the feelings that may be difficult to cope with. This is true of all of sorts of unwelcome thoughts and feelings, from envy to real psychological distress.*

History

- **Music therapy**

After World War II, musicians would go into hospitals to play music to soldiers who were wounded or who had suffered emotional trauma. In the 1950s, the

Society for Music Therapy and Remedial Music was formed. The French cellist Juliette Alvin introduced the first training course for music therapists in the late 1960s. At around the same time, Paul Nordoff and Clive Robbins published a book on music therapy in special education and initiated a training course in London; Nordoff Robbins is now a charity offering music therapy. In 1967, the Association of Professional Music Therapists (now the British Association of Music Therapists) was formed.

In 1982, the NHS recognised music therapy as an effective form of treatment.

● Art therapy

The term "art therapy" was first used in 1942 by the British artist Adrian Hill, who experienced the value of art at first hand when he was recovering from tuberculosis in a sanatorium. Other art therapy pioneers extended his work into long-stay psychiatric hospitals. In 1964, the British Association of Art Therapists was founded.

Art therapists have been inspired by theories such as psychoanalysis, attachment-based therapy and mindfulness.

● Play therapy

In the 1930s, the Austrian child psychoanalyst Melanie Klein introduced play into her analysis of children in order to explore their unconscious thoughts and feelings. From the late 1930s onwards, other workers began to use play therapy with children. The person who is considered the founder of play therapy is Virginia Axline, who developed non-directive play therapy in the United States in the 1940s. In 1964, she wrote an influential book on play therapy, *Dibs: In Search of Self,* in which she recounted the story of her work with a five-year-old boy who was withdrawn and uncommunicative. By the end of the play therapy, Dibs had found his true self and was discovered to be extremely intelligent, with an IQ of 168.

Filial therapy, which coaches parents in the use of therapeutic play techniques to use at home with their children, is a much more recent development (see below).

● Drama therapy

The roots of drama therapy can be traced back over hundreds of years – drama has long been used as a way of healing mental distress.

The founder of drama therapy was an Austrian-American psychiatrist called Jacob L Moreno. In his autobiography, Moreno recalls this encounter with Sigmund Freud, the founding father of psychoanalysis, in 1912.

> I attended one of Freud's lectures. He had just finished an analysis of a telepathic dream. As the students filed out, he singled me out from the crowd and asked me what I was doing. I responded, 'Well, Dr. Freud, I start where you leave off. You meet people in the artificial setting of your office. I meet them on the street and in their homes, in their natural surroundings. You analyse their dreams. I give them the courage to dream again. You analyse and tear them apart. I let them act out their conflicting roles and help them to put the parts back together again.

Following on from the pioneering work of Jacob Moreno, by the mid-20th century a number of people in the United States, Europe and Britain were all separately developing ways of using drama as therapy. In 1976, the British Association for Dramatherapy was founded and the first undergraduate course in drama therapy was run. Other courses followed. In 1984, the British Psychodrama Association was founded. Five years later, dramatherapists were recognised by the NHS and in 1997, drama therapy became a state registered profession.

What the therapy involves

● Music therapy

Music therapy isn't about learning to play an instrument. The child will be using simple instruments – particularly percussion instruments – in rhythmic-based activities, together with the therapist. The therapist will respond to any form of communication by the child, whether sounds made with an instrument or voice, movements or facial expression. The therapist may also use songs, either making up songs or changing the words to well-known songs so that they relate to the child. Older children and adolescents might want to compose their own music, songs or raps. They can explore troubling issues in a safe, non-threatening space through a musical and verbal dialogue with the therapist.

● Art therapy

Art therapists use all kinds of media such as crayons, paint, chalk, modelling clay, photography and collage (cutting out pictures and words and using them to form a new picture).

3

The therapist isn't there to teach people to draw or paint well or produce a great piece of artwork – it's about producing images expressing what you feel inside, rather than depicting what you see in the outside world. The idea is that adults and children can express feelings and memories through their artwork when expressing them in other ways is difficult; they can gain emotional release and new insights with the help of the art therapist. The art therapist develops a supportive relationship with them, while guiding them through the process of making art, and helps them to find meaning in and through their art. Many adolescents, for example, find it easier to express themselves by drawing or painting than to talk about their feelings – though that can become easier if they develop a relationship with the art therapist over time.

The therapist might ask the child to tell a story about the piece of art he has produced, and will help the child interpret it, teasing apart the reality and the fantasy.

● Play therapy

Play therapists use a wide range of toys and techniques including masks, puppets, dolls, sand and so on.

Play therapy may be non-directive (where the child takes the lead and decides what to do) or directive (where the therapist leads the way) or a mixture of the two. Children use toys and play figures to "act out" situations, anxieties and wishes that they can't express in words.

● Drama and storytelling therapy

Drama and storytelling can involve stories, myths, puppets, masks and improvisation, providing an indirect way of facing painful situations and emotions. For example, hearing stories about a hero or heroine who has conquered adversity can introduce a child to the idea that he too is a survivor after facing threat and danger. The therapist helps the child to create their own dramatic scenes or imaginary stories.

The sessions

Creative arts therapists work in clinical and other settings including schools (mainstream and special schools), hospitals, nurseries, child development centres, therapy centres, and adoption support organisations as well as the child's own home. They may be employed by an organisation, such as the NHS, the local authority's education service, children's services or other adoption support organisations, or be in private practice.

The therapist will usually meet with the parent(s) first, then work on their own with the child individually (or in a group) for a number of weeks or months. Therapy sessions will usually be weekly for a set time, such as an hour, and can go on for any duration depending on the child's needs. Every few weeks the therapist will meet with the parents to discuss how the sessions are going and the child's progress.

Some arts therapists who are encouraging the child to explore his or her life story will ask the parent to stay in the room. This demonstrates to the child that the parent can cope with hearing what has happened to him or her, which reassures the child and builds their confidence in his or her parent's ability to support them.

A music therapist may work with the child individually or in a group or together with the parent(s). Where parents take part in music therapy sessions, especially with young children, making music together can help build the bond between parent and child.

SENSORY INTEGRATION THERAPY

Sensory integration therapy is based on the theory that some children have difficulty in processing information from their bodily senses and the environment.

This area of therapy has met with some criticism from the occupational therapy profession, and some people in the medical profession are unsure about using sensory processing disorder as a diagnosis and question whether sensory processing difficulties are an actual disorder of the sensory pathways of the brain. However, sensory integration therapy is offered in the UK and is covered by the Adoption Support Fund in England.

Core principles

The brain needs to organise information it receives from the input from our senses: touch, hearing, sight, taste and smell. In addition, there are two other senses: vestibular (relating to movement and balance) and proprioception (the joints and muscles sensing where the parts of your body are and what they are doing). Responding to and interpreting this information is known as sensory integration. When sensory integration does not develop as it should, it interferes with children's ability to play, learn, pay attention in school and cope with daily life.

Sensory processing or sensory integration disorders can take the form of either under- or over-responsiveness to information coming from the senses.

Dysfunction in sensory integration is sometimes found in children who have conditions such as autism, cerebral palsy and attention deficit hyperactivity disorder, but some people believe that trauma and neglectful early life experiences can also damage the ability to process sensory information. It might result from a lack of stimulation and missing out on the usual experiences of moving around and playing – for example, a child might have spent long hours strapped in a high chair or buggy as a baby or toddler.

Sensations such as sounds, smells and touch that most children would not even notice can seem overwhelming to a child with a disorder of sensory integration. The child may seem "out of touch" with what is going on in his body, for example, he may appear to be unaware of whether he is hungry or full, or whether he is hot or cold – he might go outside on a freezing day without a coat and apparently not feel cold. He may appear not to hear things. He may be extremely sensitive to sound and find a noisy environment stressful or be easily distracted by a background noise such as a clock ticking. He may seem hypersensitive to touch and find his clothes scratchy and uncomfortable. Certain tastes or smells that others would barely notice, make him feel ill.

Being on a crowded bus or in a noisy classroom can be overwhelming and extremely stressful. Some children, on the other hand, seek out particular sensations. This may lead to behaviours such as constant rocking on their chair, which can be misinterpreted by the teacher as naughtiness and lead to them being told off. "Motor planning" can also be affected, which means children may appear clumsy, drop things, fall over a lot and have poor co-ordination, making it harder for them to master skills such as throwing and catching a ball, kicking a football, or using a pencil or cutlery.

Some children develop behaviours to help them ease the discomfort or to escape from something in the environment that is bothering them, and this behaviour may appear odd or be difficult for others to understand. For example, if the child finds the taste of toothpaste much too strong, she will refuse to clean her teeth. If she hates the sound or the smell of the toilets at nursery or school, she may soil herself rather than use the toilet.

Proponents of sensory integration theory believe that deficient sensory processing is a developmental disorder that can be helped by therapy. Sensory integration therapy and sensory processing therapy aim to improve the way the child functions in terms of sensory integration and also to help those around him to develop strategies and make adaptations so that everyday activities are less stressful and difficult for him. Once a child has become more able to tune in to his physical sensations, he may be more ready and able to engage with psychological therapies.

History

Dr A Jean Ayres, an American occupational therapist and clinical psychologist born in 1920, developed the theory of sensory integration and how sensation affects learning, social-emotional development and other processes such as motor performance and attention.

Since she first described sensory integration dysfunction in the 1970s, sensory-based therapies have been used increasingly, mainly by occupational therapists.

In the UK and Ireland, there were four professional organisations working in this field from the late 1970s onwards, and in 1994 they came together to form the Sensory Integration Network UK and Ireland. This is a not-for-profit membership organisation open to occupational therapists, physiotherapists and other professionals, parents and carers with an interest in sensory integration. The Sensory Integration Network has developed a master's level training course as well as a number of other training courses for therapists.

What the therapy involves

Therapists use materials like sand, dough, water and rice as well as toys and objects with different textures to introduce children to different tactile sensations or to help them get used to the feelings these materials evoke. The therapist may use substances with different smells and tastes. He/she may also work with sounds, using toys that squeak or make other noises and involve the child in singing and clapping rhymes and listening to or making music.

For some children whose problems are to do with balance and co-ordination and being aware of where their body is, therapists recommend activities to stimulate movement or help the child develop new skills involving movement like bouncing balls, skipping, rocking, throwing beanbags and playing catch.

Some children respond well to feeling physical pressure against their body, with therapists recommending to parents that the child wears a weighted belt or vest or sleeps under heavy blankets. Therapists may also recommend ways to help children regulate themselves or reach a comfortable level of stimulation in their day-to-day life – this may involve something like a walk or jumping on a trampoline, or it may involve something that calms the child down like listening to gentle music.

An occupational therapist – Patricia Wilbarger – introduced a technique that involves brushing the child's body at regular intervals with a soft brush in order to "desensitise" the child to touch. This brushing programme, which is sometimes included in a treatment programme, is called the Wilbarger protocol.

The sessions

The therapist will first carry out an assessment of the child's sensory needs. Through interviews and questionnaires, he/she will gather information from the child's parent(s) and perhaps also the teacher(s) about how the child performs in daily life.

The therapist will set up activities and tests of motor functioning for the child to look at how the child responds and determine where his sensory difficulties lie and what type of intervention and exercises would be helpful. The therapist also helps to work out what kind of environments and sensations make the child feel most comfortable.

Therapy often takes place one to one with the child. Activities are chosen to appeal to the individual child and to provide opportunities for him to become better at coping with environmental challenges.

As well as the sessions with the child, therapists usually also work with the child's parent(s) and others in the child's life to help them understand their child's sensory needs and to find ways to support him at home and school. The therapist will suggest strategies that the child, parent and teacher can use to adapt to and compensate for his dysfunction, such as reducing distraction in the classroom, providing alternative activities for those that are too stimulating or stressful, and ways of helping the child to self-regulate and feel "just right".

PARENT AND CHILD PLAY THERAPIES

Theraplay and filial play therapy both differ from traditional play therapy. Instead of waiting outside while the therapist works with their child, parents conduct the play therapy sessions themselves. The key person is the adult who is already important to that child, and it is the relationship with the parent – not the therapist – that brings about therapeutic change. These therapies can be seen as a blend between family therapy and play therapy.

Theraplay®

Core principles

Theraplay is a type of play therapy in which the parent leads games and activities with their child in a structured way for a set amount of time each week. The games and activities are chosen to bring about connection and to be fun, building attachment and strengthening the trust and the relationship between the parent and child.

The playful interaction that parents learn to lead during the sessions can be incorporated into daily life and routines to bring their children closer, both physically and emotionally. The idea is that the child feels loved, cared for and more secure.

In Theraplay the therapist coaches and guides the parent in how to tune into their child and adjust the play to the child's needs. The child plays with the parent rather than with toys or play figures. In contrast to traditional play therapy, with its interpretation of symbolic play and focus on the child's inner thoughts and feelings, Theraplay is based on non-verbal communication so it can be used with younger children and those with developmental delays.

This type of therapy is claimed to be particularly suitable for addressing early life trauma and attachment disorders.

The Theraplay Institute in the US says:

> Trauma such as neglect which occurs before the child can speak remains in the non-conscious realm of the child's brain and cannot readily come to light. Because Theraplay incorporates positive relationship experiences that the child missed as a baby, children who have experienced early loss

or trauma can integrate these new experiences more effectively than with non-directive, symbolic therapies. Theraplay helps parent and child create healthy real-time experiences together that can heal the trauma of the past.

3

History

In the US, in the late 1960s, clinical psychologist Ann Jernberg became the Director of Psychological Services for the new Chicago Head Start programme, which aimed to promote children's mental health. Together with her assistant Phyllis Booth she created her own programme and trained people to go into schools and work with children who needed help. This evolved into Theraplay.

The Theraplay Institute was formed in 1971. In the 1980s, the Institute began training others to use Theraplay and today Theraplay is used in many countries around the world including the UK. Its focus has shifted towards the child–caregiver relationship and promoting secure attachment.

What the therapy involves

To begin with, the therapist will interview the parent to find out about the child and then carry out an assessment using something called the Marschak Interaction Method (MIM). Parents are asked to complete a series of tasks with their child while they are observed – and may also be filmed – by the therapist for around 30 to 60 minutes. The therapist looks at how the caregiver and the child interact in these tasks, the strengths of the adult and child, and their relationship. The therapist also looks at the child's ability to respond to the parent's efforts. After getting to know the parent and child, the therapist will teach the parent about the Theraplay activities and the recommended programme to use with the child.

The actual play sessions are designed around four dimensions. These are:

- Structure – relating to the parent's ability to set limits and provide an appropriately ordered environment
- Engagement – engaging the child in interaction while being attuned to his or her state of arousal or emotional state
- Nurture – meeting the child's needs for attention, soothing and care
- Challenge – supporting and encouraging the child to achieve at a developmentally appropriate level.

For example, an activity that the parent could do with the child to promote structure might be something like *Simon Says*; promoting nurture could be rocking the child or giving her a massage; and challenge could mean getting the child to climb a tower of pillows.

The therapist guides the parent during the session, coaching him or her to tune in to the child and to adjust activities to the child's needs for structure, engagement, nurture and challenge, within the context of playful interaction, physical games and fun.

The sessions

The initial sessions will generally be held in the therapist's own play room but after that parents can continue with regular Theraplay sessions at home. Each session lasts around 30 minutes. Every few sessions, the therapist meets with the parent without the child present, to discuss progress and goals. The total number of sessions varies depending on the child's needs. For example, it could be 20 sessions or more, with four follow-up sessions over the next year.

The Theraplay Institute says that, once the child has formed a bond of attachment with the parents, eventually he or she might need to process the past using other types of therapy such as Dyadic Developmental Psychotherapy (see pp55–8). Some therapists are trained in both Theraplay and DDP and are experienced in combining these.

Filial therapy

Core principles

As with Theraplay, the idea of filial therapy is that the best adult to work with a child is the parent, not the therapist. Instead of the child developing a new relationship with a therapist, therapists train parents to carry out special play sessions with their children in order to build on and strengthen the relationship between parent and child.

Filial therapy is a child-centred approach based on non-directive play therapy principles – in other words, the child (within limits) decides how he or she would like to play.

Parents learn the skills of filial therapy from experienced therapists who supervise them directly at first and then indirectly and they can adapt the skills to use in everyday family life.

The therapist is also there to support parents with their own emotional needs and stress, and to build their confidence in their ability to help the child.

History

Filial therapy was developed in the US in the 1960s as a branch of play therapy by Louise and Bernard Guerney. Louise Guerney is Professor of Human Development and Counselling Psychology at Penn State University in the US. She has trained and supervised hundreds of professionals in this model of family therapy.

What the therapy involves

Parents are coached in special skills that enable them to respond empathically to the needs of the child, expressed through play. The therapist will, at first, demonstrate these with the child and give the parents the chance to develop their skills through role play.

During filial therapy sessions, the child leads the play. No pressure is put on the child to do or talk about anything he or she doesn't want to. While sitting alongside and watching the child play, parents are asked to use a special technique that involves commenting on or describing what the child is doing, but without asking questions, giving instructions or trying to teach the child. The aim of this is to make children feel accepted, valued and heard by the parent (and not judged). Most children enjoy this concentrated form of attention from their parent and it is said to make for a more positive relationship between parent and child.

As in play therapy, children can use play to work through some of their difficult emotions rather than "internalising" them and becoming withdrawn, or "externalising" them and lashing out or being destructive. The parent learns particular skills in order to make the play therapeutic for their child: structuring skills, empathic listening skills, imaginative skills and limit-setting. For example, if the parent sets limits (e.g. the child mustn't break the toys or the session will have to be cut short) the child learns that his or her actions have consequences.

The sessions

Filial play therapy is suitable for children from three to around 13.

The therapist will assess the child and family and then typically spend three weeks training the parents in filial skills, in weekly sessions lasting about an hour. (Sometimes parents learn about filial therapy in a group format rather than individually.)

If there are two parents in the family, both of them can be trained so that they can carry out the play sessions. If there's more than one child in the family, it's a good idea for each child to have a filial play session or at least some "special time" with a parent.

The first few sessions of filial play with the child are likely to take place in the therapist's playroom but after that the parent can continue them at home for 30 minutes every week at the same time. If possible, the therapist will observe the session (or a recording of the session) and discuss it with the parent afterwards. The therapist will probably meet with the parents once a week at first but then this might change to fortnightly or monthly.

Filial therapy usually takes three to six months to complete, with some follow-up sessions. Parents can continue the sessions at home for as long as they want or as long as they feel their child is benefiting.

Dyadic developmental psychotherapy (DDP)

DDP is a type of psychotherapy for children and young people with complex psychological problems, who have failed to establish secure attachments with their adoptive parents. Some children are reluctant to go to their adoptive parents for comfort, support and help. They may be particularly self-reliant, find relationships difficult, and have a strong need to control everything in their environment, including their parents.

DDP therapists can work with children as young as three, and occasionally even with two-year-olds. With the parents always being in the room and attunement being a core component of DDP, children can become actively involved from a young age. DDP therapists use a wide range of non-verbal components such as play, puppets and drawing in addition to words. They also help parents regulate their child using physical actions such as rocking, using rhythm and touch.

Core principles

The core principle of DDP is to help adopted children to recover from early trauma by establishing interactions with their adoptive parents that enable the child to feel safe and connected and which build new, stronger attachments between them. In DDP there is a focus on developing and maintaining strong, emotionally attuned relationships between therapist, parent and child. With this type of therapy, parents gain new understanding of their child's behaviour and responses, tune in to his or her emotional experiences, and learn how to nurture attachment – which in turn helps the child to feel safe and build trust.

Parents are actively involved in the sessions. The therapist helps them to parent with an attitude based on five key principles: playfulness, acceptance, curiosity and empathy (PACE) as well as love. They learn ways of containing their child's emotions and behaviours.

Parents can continue to use the therapeutic parenting techniques at home as well as during the sessions.

History

In the 1980s, American clinical psychologist Dan Hughes developed a model for treating children who had been traumatised by their attachment figures. He called it dyadic developmental psychotherapy because children's development depends on and is highly influenced by the nature of the parent–child relationship, which requires ongoing dyadic (reciprocal) experiences between them. He began training practitioners in the UK in 2000, and there are now dozens of practitioners offering DDP.

DDP is taught in Canada and, to a lesser extent, in other countries as well as the US and the UK.

Hughes set up the DDP Institute, of which he is President, in the US in 2009. The DDP Network is a worldwide body that promotes DDP and provides information on the therapy and how to train to become a certified practitioner. The therapy has been taken up by other parenting experts in the UK, such as Kim Golding, and is now well-known and fairly widely available in the UK.

What the therapy involves

DDP is family-based. It is both a psychological therapy in which a therapist works with an individual family over the course of a number of sessions, and a parenting model that can be taught to a group of adoptive parents in a workshop setting.

Parents learn the principles of parenting with PACE, as described by Dan Hughes:

> *Eye contact, voice tone, touch, movement and gestures are actively employed to communicate safety, acceptance, curiosity, playfulness and empathy, and never threat or coercion.*

> *Opportunities for enjoyment and laughter, play and fun are provided unconditionally throughout every day with the child.*

> *The child's symptoms or problems are accepted and contained. The child is shown how these simply reflect his history. They are often associated with shame which must be reduced by the adult's response to the behaviour.*

> *The child's resistance to parenting and treatment interventions is responded to with acceptance, curiosity and empathy.*

The sessions

The therapist will use the first sessions to work with the parents, exploring the impact that parenting the child is having on them, and preparing them for their role in the therapeutic process and future sessions involving the child. When the therapist judges the parents are ready, the child will join the sessions.

The sessions involving the child explore his or her experience and feelings. The therapist and child will build a new "narrative" (they may do this by talking or by using something like puppets or drawing) that helps the child understand how feelings and behaviour are linked to past experiences. The therapist will help the child communicate with the parents – perhaps speaking "for" the child to tell parents what he or she would want them to know – and supports the child to manage his or her emotions.

The aim is to help children feel that they are lovable, that they deserve to be loved by good parents, and that they are part of their adoptive family.

According to the DDP Network:

> *Therapy will end when:*

> * *The therapist and parents think that the child is developing some attachment security within the family*

- *Family members can continue the process of being emotionally available and intersubjectively connected without the help of the therapist.*

This can be a long process because of the level of fear that the child has about being parented.

Some therapists will offer breaks in therapy when it is felt that this will be helpful for the child. Sometimes breaks are because the parents need more intensive support because of the challenges that they are experiencing.

Courses of therapy for individual families are offered by practitioners who are trained therapists and who have received additional training and supervision to provide DDP as a therapy. The DDP parenting model is also often taught in group workshops offered by adoption support organisations and led by people who may either be therapists or social workers who have had additional training and supervision to apply the principles of DDP to working with families.

EYE MOVEMENT DESENSITISATION AND REPROCESSING THERAPY (EMDR)™

Core principles

EMDR is a procedure that is used with adults and children experiencing post-traumatic stress, particularly when the memory of the traumatic event(s) is causing flashbacks, nightmares, panic attacks and so on. The theory behind EMDR is that the brain has stored the traumatic memory together with the emotions the person experienced at the time of the event, and that the brain needs to be able to "process" the memory of the trauma so that the person can recall the events without becoming distressed or anxious.

Long-term memories have a physical presence in the brain – when a new long-term memory is formed, neurons make new physical connections with each other. This happens in a part of the brain called the hippocampus, which prioritises information that has a strong emotional component. As more memories are formed, the neurons representing memories that have been consolidated migrate away from the hippocampus and further into the cortex.

Proponents of EMDR claim that this can be achieved for traumatic memories by the technique of "bilateral stimulation" (see below). Some EMDR practitioners also use it for other issues such as attachment disorders, dissociation and difficulties with self-regulation.

EMDR may be used on its own or it may precede or be used alongside other therapies, such as a creative therapy or play therapy.

History

In the 1980s, American psychologist Dr Francine Shapiro developed a theory that trauma results in a "frozen state" in the brain and that rapid eye movements unblock this state and allow the information to be processed. In 1990, she set up the EMDR Institute in California, which offers training for practitioners in how to carry out EMDR. Since then, the scope of EMDR has evolved and it includes things other than rapid eye movements – such as sound and touch.

EMDR therapists claim that the bilateral stimulation given during EMDR helps the brain to process the traumatic memory. But there has been – and still is – some controversy over how it works. It should be noted that EMDR has elements reminiscent of other therapies, e.g. a relaxation effect and "exposure", in the way in which the client re-tells the story or feels their way through their fear in a safe and supported setting that can help dissipate painful feelings.

What the therapy involves

EMDR therapy requires the client to be quiet, rather than speaking. Dr Francine Shapiro has described it like this:

> During memory reprocessing, the client recalls a disturbing event for a short period (for example, 30 seconds) while simultaneously undergoing bilateral stimulation that can consist of moving the eyes from side to side, vibrations or tapping movements on different sides of the body, or tones delivered through one ear, then the other, via headphones. New associations emerge and often become the new focus of attention. No homework is required, and the client is not asked to describe the memory in detail. The goal is to let the brain's information processing system make new internal connections as the client focuses on the thoughts, emotions, memories and other associations that are freely made during the sets of bilateral stimulation.

The client is asked to think of the traumatic event and concentrate on it while following the therapist's instructions to, for example, track his or her finger rapidly with their eyes as the therapist moves it from side to side in front of their face, about 30cm away. Or the therapist may use a light for the person to track, or may tap one side of the person's body, or snap their fingers on either side of their head.

The sessions

The therapist will start by asking about the adult's or child's problems/traumatic events.

Then the therapist will apply the "bilateral stimulation". If there are a number of events from the past that need to be addressed, the therapist will agree with the client on the order in which to do this over the course of several sessions.

The therapist will discuss with parents the child's progress during the therapy, and the number of sessions will depend on progress made.

DIALECTICAL BEHAVIOUR THERAPY (DBT)

This is a specific kind of cognitive behaviour therapy that combines behaviour therapy with elements of acceptance and mindfulness, derived from Buddhist meditative practice. It is designed to help people who have problems managing difficult and painful emotions or who have developed unhelpful "coping strategies".

NICE (National Institute for Health and Care Excellence) recognises DBT as an effective treatment for self-harm in women with borderline personality disorder (a condition that often involves impulsive behaviour, problems with relationships, emotional dysregulation, self-harm and suicidal thoughts or attempts at suicide).

DBT is also sometimes used with other conditions such as depression, post-traumatic stress disorder, emotional dysregulation, eating disorders and ADHD, and with people who have been sexually abused.

Core principles

This therapy focuses on both acceptance and change. The term "dialectical" refers to finding a balance between two things: accepting yourself (or your situation or your feelings) and changing your harmful behaviour.

Because they are often working with people who have particularly severe problems, most DBT therapists work in teams and have a team meeting each week to discuss their work and increase their effectiveness.

History

Dialectical behaviour therapy was developed in the US in the late 1970s by Marsha Linehan, Professor of Psychology at the University of Washington. She went on to set up the Linehan Institute, a non-profit organisation to promote the therapy, and BehavioralTech, a DBT training and consultancy company that provides training to mental health care providers and treatment teams.

It is now used across the US and increasingly in Europe.

In the UK, some NHS services offer DBT, including its use for children and adolescents. British Isles DBT Training is the only provider of DBT training to practitioners in Great Britain and the Republic of Ireland, and has been training DBT teams in the UK since 1997. There are now over 360 DBT programmes in the UK. There are also a number of therapists in private practice, though they may not be able to offer the group skills training.

What the therapy involves

DBT is about problem-solving. Therapists look at behaviours, identify what is going on, teach skills and develop solutions that can help their client learn to manage painful emotions and lead a more settled life.

There are four key skills:

* Mindfulness (paying attention to the present moment, non-judgmentally and with perspective)

* Distress tolerance (learning to bear pain rather than being overwhelmed by it or hiding from it)

* Emotion regulation (learning to identify your emotions and calm yourself when you are angry, frustrated or anxious)

- Interpersonal effectiveness (e.g. learning effective strategies for asking for what you need and coping with conflict).

Clients develop these skills in group training sessions. Another element is telephone coaching, which helps clients who are in crisis or who need advice on putting the skills into practice.

There are variations on the therapy that are designed to target certain difficulties more specifically – such as disorders of over-control and eating disorders. There are also variations for use with dysregulated and suicidal older children and adolescents involving skills training groups for families as well as individual therapy and coaching by phone, email and/or text.

The sessions

Clients are given both individual therapy and training in groups (led by two therapists).

Individual therapy sessions are held one-to-one, each week, for around 50 to 60 minutes. The group element involves training in the four key skills of DBT by two therapists for two hours each time. There will also be homework tasks to complete between sessions.

EQUINE-ASSISTED THERAPY[1]

Therapy involving horses is used with a range of mental health needs such as behavioural issues, attention deficit disorder, abuse, trauma, depression, anxiety and relationship problems.

Horses may have a strong motivational attraction for some children and for others learning to relate to a horse may be highly therapeutic – especially their powerful presence and the behaviours that need to be a part of learning about horses. Some parents find that the offer of this form of intervention is the only therapy that the child will accept. Equine-assisted therapy is not the same as learning to ride a horse.

---

1 Equine therapy is currently not funded by the ASF; this is due to be reviewed.

Core principles

Equine-assisted therapy involves the child taking part in activities with horses with the assistance of a therapist. Children can learn important things about themselves and others when the therapist guides them in understanding the relationship they need to develop with the horse and the challenges involved. People who provide and use equine therapy believe it can help self-confidence, self-esteem, communication, relationships, problem-solving, coping skills and personal responsibility. Equine-assisted therapy is not to be confused with the "riding for the disabled" movement, where the focus is on promoting strength, balance, co-ordination and motor skills in children and adults with physical disabilities.

Equine-assisted *learning* is also slightly different. The emphasis here is on using horses to achieve educational goals, for example, with children with social, emotional or behavioural difficulties who find it hard to engage with a traditional school setting. As well as hands-on work with horses and working in a group to encourage social skills and develop confidence, the ability to follow instructions and so on, learners can tackle curriculum subjects by relating them to horses and equine care.

History

In the UK, equine therapy was first used in Norfolk in around 1990 by Ruth McMahon, a senior occupational therapist who worked with community mental health teams in the Norfolk and Suffolk Mental Health NHS Trust. Initially, clients with mental health problems were encouraged to attend a local riding school to build confidence. They consistently reported feeling better after their riding sessions, so McMahon explored the possibilities of extending the therapeutic benefits and equine therapy is now offered by a number of centres in the UK.

The approach is widely used in the US, where there is a thriving equine therapy scene. The Equine Assisted Growth & Learning Association (EAGALA) was founded in the US in 1999 and now has branches in 49 countries around the world. It is a non-profit-making professional association that offers training, certification for trainers, and membership services. There are EAGALA groups in London, the north of England, Cumbria and the Scottish Borders, the south-west and the Midlands.

In the UK there is a framework for training and accrediting equine-assisted *learning* facilitators developed by Tricia Day who founded Equine Assisted Qualifications. There are a number of approved equine-assisted learning centres, some of which specialise in certain areas such as adults in recovery from drug or alcohol misuse or children and young people with autism spectrum conditions.

What the therapy involves

In equine-assisted therapy, no actual riding is involved. The therapy provides an opportunity to spend time outside with horses and to experience the connection and trust that a human can develop with a horse.

To start with, the child or young person will learn about safety issues around horses. Then they will observe the horses and how they interact with each other and will be prompted to think about why they behave the way they do. The child will touch and stroke the horses and, as he or she develops confidence, the therapist may ask him or her to do certain activities with a horse, such as grooming it, leading it to a particular place or putting a halter on it. The therapist may also ask the child to build structures in the field, using props, and then lead the horse through or around these.

Therapists may also use metaphors based on the horse's behaviour and responses to help the young person achieve new insights into their own responses. They also take a problem-solving approach – for example, if the horse refuses to co-operate or avoids an obstacle and the young person becomes angry and walks away, they will encourage him to explore the horse's reaction and to find another solution.

The sessions

Sessions may be in groups or individual. Equine-assisted therapy sessions are led by both a therapist (a mental health professional) and a horse specialist.

THERAPEUTIC LIFE STORY WORK

Providing a life story book for adopted children (and a later life letter for the child to be given when he or she is older) became a statutory requirement for adoption agencies in England in December 2005 and is considered to be good practice elsewhere in the UK. For very young children who are being adopted, social workers put together a book with information, photographs and other mementoes of the child's early life and the people and places in it. Older children who are going to be (or have been) adopted can be involved in this and work with an adult to collect and organise the information.

This work helps the child understand their identity, to know about their birth family (and why they cannot live with their birth parents and/or, sometimes, siblings) and to have a record of what has happened in their life so far, such as living with extended family members or foster carers.

However, the life story book will need to develop and be worked on over the course of time as children and young people need and want to explore new questions and thoughts and feelings, with the life story work having a therapeutic focus.

Therapeutic life story work is covered by the Adoption Support Fund.

Core principles

Therapeutic life story work is undertaken with adopted children and young people who need help in understanding their past and its impact on the present. This can include addressing their thoughts, feelings and emotions about their experiences and their birth family. Therapeutic life story work can be undertaken with adolescents who want to know more detail about their past or who are keen to have a reunion with birth relatives and need help to prepare for this. It can also help where a young person is angry and expressing their anger in ways that are putting their relationship and home life with their adopters at risk.

Children may have little explicit memory of events or people from their early life (especially if they were adopted at a young age) and many looked after and adopted children are confused about what happened to them and why.

The child may have developed an internal narrative about herself that says: 'I am a bad person', 'I am unlovable' or 'It was my fault that I was adopted'. He may have internalised ideas about others that say 'People who care for me hurt me and let me down' or he may expect that he will be moved on from his adoptive parents just as he has been moved on from other carers before. So the therapist aims to correct misconceptions, help the child process what has happened, and construct a more positive narrative.

If there are painful and distressing events that they need to hear about and come to terms with, working with a therapist to discuss and reflect on their story may help them to make sense of it and manage their complex feelings. Therapeutic life story work aims to help young people to develop a more settled perspective on negative emotions.

It is the process of doing this work, rather than the end product in the form of a life story book, film or whatever, that is the most valuable part.

History

Life story books have been completed for looked after and adopted children for many years but were often not as helpful as they might have been.

In the 1990s, children's social worker Joy Rees began looking at ways to make life story books better and she came up with a new approach. Instead of beginning the book with the child's birth and following his life chronologically, she suggested starting the child's story in the present – his life with his adoptive parents – then going back to the past, then returning to the present before looking ahead to the future. This aims to give the child a greater feeling of security and sense of belonging in his new adoptive family. Ryan and Walker first addressed this in their guide, *Making Life Story Books*, published by BAAF in 1985. Since then, practice has developed in this area and life story work has also embraced the use of electronic multimedia options, but tried and tested techniques remain. The latest edition of this work is titled *Life Story Work: Why, What, How and When*, and has been published by CoramBAAF in 2016.

Life story work began to be used, in some traumatised children, as a form of therapy as well as a way of understanding their identity and history. As social work practice began to change, workers such as Polly Baynes, Tony Ryan and Rodger Walker looked at ways to make life story work more therapeutic.

Therapeutic life story work for traumatised children has developed further with the work of Richard Rose, Associate Professor of Social Work and Social Policy at La Trobe University, Melbourne, Australia, Fellow of the Berry Street Childhood Institute, Australia, and Director of Child Trauma Intervention Services Ltd in the UK. Professor Rose develops academic training programmes in the UK and internationally, and is in the process of setting up a professional body, Therapeutic Life Story Work International (www.childtraumaintervention. com/therapeutic-life-story-work-international.php).

Dr Simon Hammond and Dr Neil Cooper from the University of East Anglia have developed life story work explicitly focusing on how computers and digital technologies (rather than painting pictures and sticking photographs into a scrapbook) can be used in life story work, particularly with adolescents (Hammond and Cooper, 2013).

3

What the therapy involves

There are different approaches, depending on the age and level of understanding of the child and the therapist's individual way of working. Some therapists will incorporate techniques from play therapy and art therapy. As developed by Richard Rose, therapeutic life story work involves the adoptive parent working in a triad with the child and the practitioner. They explore the child's history and feelings together. This helps the adoptive parent to have a better understanding of their child. The therapist will help the child to understand how the impact of his past experiences and relationships might be affecting him and his behaviour in the present.

It can also be helpful for a child to see that their adoptive parent has heard some of the awful things that they have witnessed or experienced, and that their parent can acknowledge that. It can help the child to feel contained and protected, and may strengthen attachment.

The sessions

Therapists work with children and their adoptive parents in their home. Children and young people between the ages of four and 17 can benefit. Typically the direct work with child and parent takes place in a one-hour session each fortnight over a nine- to 12-month period.

Early in the process, the therapist will gather information about the child from a range of different people and sources. Then he or she will help the child to explore it, alongside the parent. The child records their thoughts, feelings and emotions, for example, on a long roll of wallpaper. In the final sessions, the child decides what will be included in their life story book, and the book is written with the help of the therapist.

Especially with older children and young people, some life story work therapists use new digital technologies such as video clips and music – for example, the young person could make a film of herself walking around significant places from her past and explaining what they mean to her. These videos provide the basis for supportive conversations with the therapist that can help the young person make sense of her past.

THERAPEUTIC PARENTING APPROACHES AND PARENTING SKILLS GROUPS

Parenting a traumatised child is not the same as parenting other children. Adopted children's disordered attachment, developmental trauma and other problems can manifest themselves in powerful and uncontrolled emotional outbursts, anger, difficulty bonding with their new parents, lying and other "difficult" behaviour. Some are diagnosed with ADHD (attention deficit hyperactivity disorder). Children struggle at home and school and parents can suffer immense stress and trauma themselves.

Experts in the neuroscience of trauma warn that traditional behaviour management strategies may not be effective for traumatised children and indeed may cause further distress. They argue that, in any case, problematic behaviour is often simply a manifestation of the difficulty that many traumatised children have in managing overwhelming stress and feelings of shame.

The neuroscience-based approach

In relation to ADHD, for example, Dr Bruce Perry of the Child Trauma Academy in the US (quoted in Boffey, 2014) has said that he favours an approach going back to what he calls the root causes of the problem and often requires attention being focused on the parents:

> There are a number of non-pharmacological therapies which have been pretty effective. A lot of them involve helping the adults that are around children...

> Part of what happens if you have an anxious, overwhelmed child is that it becomes contagious. When a child is struggling, the adults around them are easily dysregulated too. This negative feedback process between the frustrated teacher or parent and dysregulated child can escalate out of control.

> You can teach the adults how to regulate themselves, how to have realistic expectations of the children, how to give them opportunities that are achievable and have success and coach them through the process of helping children who are struggling.

> There are a lot of therapeutic approaches. Some would use somato-sensory therapies like yoga, some use motor activity like drumming.

Perry argues that the brain organises from the bottom to the top, with the lower parts of the brain (the brain stem or "survival brain") developing much earlier than the cortical areas, or "thinking brain"; trauma and neglect in early life affect the developing brain in such a way that the "thinking brain" does not function properly and, under any kind of stress, the child goes into "fight or flight" mode and is unable to think clearly. Children who constantly feel scared and threatened require special responses. Perry claims that you need to change the neural networks by regulating the lower parts of the brain, and believes that this can be achieved via repetitive, rhythmic activities such as singing, dancing, swinging, bouncing on a trampoline, massage and grooming animals. This, he says, will have the effect of regulating anxiety and stress, calming the child so that you can then go on to use other things such as positive relationships, rewards and sanctions or talking therapies.

Perry has called his model of brain function and parenting approach the "Neurosequential Model of Therapeutics". It claims to analyse what the "neurological damage" has been, looks at the child's development and then creates developmentally-appropriate interventions and enrichment activities to meet the individual child's needs. Later in the treatment process, when the child is functioning better, treatment recommendations would shift to more insight-orientated and cognitive-behavioural interventions.

Perry has visited the UK to speak at conferences and his work has been influential – you can read accounts from two adopters of hearing him speak about his approach (see Section 5). Many other experts, both in the UK and the US, offer training underpinned by ideas about the neuroscience of trauma and attachment.

Behaviour management with traumatised children

Typical reward–punishment strategies are hard for developmentally traumatised children to manage – the stress and shame of being "told off" may be overwhelming, and "punishments", such as time-out, evoke distressing memories for some children who have been maltreated. Traditional parenting advice tells parents to use praise and rewards to shape children's behaviour. The use of praise and rewards is important with adopted children too, of course – but children who feel overwhelming shame or have low self-esteem because of their early life experiences may not be motivated by praise and rewards in the same way as other children. In fact, as experts point out, these children may experience praise as stressful or overwhelming; this can lead them to torpedo any positive interactions because they feel they are somehow undeserving.

So a number of parenting programmes have been developed specifically to support adoptive parents and others who are parenting children who have experienced trauma and maltreatment. As well as the content of the course being targeted to adoptive parents, the course leaders have a good understanding of adoption issues and the kind of difficulties that arise.

There are a number of differing parenting training and support programmes but they share some common aims. They help parents to understand the impact of trauma and attachment difficulties on their child and help them parent the child in a therapeutic way, i.e. a way that will help the child to feel more secure, build trust and attachment and foster resilience. They also aim to give parents skills to manage "difficult" behaviour in a way that is appropriate for their child, within the context of therapeutic parenting. Parents who have attended such parenting programmes often report that they have a greater understanding of their child and feel more confident.

A one-to-one parenting skills programme called VIPP-SD has been recommended by NICE as an intervention for children with attachment difficulties soon after placement (see pp71–74).

Most of these parenting courses are conducted as group training courses presenting both theoretical ideas and practical suggestions with a range of group activities, space for personal reflection, and "homework" tasks. Adopters often find it helpful to meet others going through similar experiences and to realise that they are not alone. Courses like this also provide a breathing space for adoptive parents to stop and think about how they can and must look after their own mental health needs as well as those of their children.

When a parenting course is not enough

Increasing parents' skills and confidence can be helpful but may not be the answer for every adoptive family. Adopters struggling with seriously disturbed and violent behaviour from their children may not thank social workers for suggesting that they need help with their parenting skills.

In Professor Julie Selwyn's study (2015), some adoptive families whose adoption had broken down reported that they kept being offered the same package of parenting classes when the child's behaviours were becoming more and more difficult to manage.

It was not that parenting courses were discounted – many parents had found them useful when difficulties began to emerge. The problem was that the same parenting courses continued to be offered, as the child's behaviour grew more extreme and out of control. Parents thought that social workers were failing to understand just how desperate they were...

(Selwyn *et al*, 2015, p175)

Some children's difficulties are so serious that they require more intensive specialist therapy or therapies. Their parents may also need additional support, such as therapy for themselves or respite care to give the family some rest or a breathing space.

SOME PARENTING COURSES AND PROGRAMMES

Video-feedback Intervention to promote Positive Parenting and Sensitive Discipline (VIPP-SD)

This is a preventive programme that aims to build strong attachment relationships between parents and children and to help parents to develop sensitive ways of managing their child's behaviour. Using video to record and analyse interactions between parent and child, practitioners deliver sessions in the family home over a period of months.

Core principles

VIPP-SD is based on attachment theory and also uses some behavioural principles to help parents build strong bonds with their children and to prevent or reduce behavioural problems in children. It has a strong evidence base.

The programme is used in families with children aged from around one up to six. It is most effective when a child has been placed for at least three months but less than 12 months (before behaviours have become fixed).

Sensitive parenting can improve the parent–child relationship and the interactions between parent and child.

The Centre for Child and Family Studies at the University of Leiden in the Netherlands developed this intervention. It says:

> *Research shows that there are two aspects of parenting that play an important role in the development and continuation of behavioural problems in children: sensitivity and discipline. Sensitivity in parenting means noticing the child's signals, interpreting these signals correctly and responding to them promptly and appropriately. Discipline means setting boundaries and regulating unruly or disobedient behaviour... The combination of these two aspects is the basis of VIPP-SD, in which sensitivity in the broad sense, as well as sensitive discipline, are central themes. Basic assumptions of the intervention are creating a positive atmosphere, recognising the caregiver as the expert of (sic) the child, and emphasising and reinforcing positive interactions between caregiver and child.*

A video recording is a powerful way for both practitioner and parent to identify reactions and pick up signals that might not otherwise be spotted.

History

VIPP-SD was developed by leading researchers in attachment at the Centre for Child and Family Studies at Leiden University in the Netherlands, where it has been tested over a number of years with different groups of parents and children at risk. It is now being used with adoptive families and is offered to all adopters in the Netherlands. Research is being conducted to adapt VIPP-SD to different target groups, including families with a child with autism, staff in day care centres and children's homes and other countries including the UK, USA, Australia, Finland, Portugal, Israel and Kenya.

The Tavistock & Portman NHS Trust is the centre of VIPP-SD training in the UK. It has been using this intervention since 2014 and is now rolling it out more widely – it is working with TACT Adoption and Fostering and others to deliver it to adoptive families.

NICE – the National Institute for Health and Care Excellence – is the UK body that assesses the scientific evidence for various treatments, therapies and interventions used in a range of medical and psychological problems and makes recommendations about which ones should be used and funded. Because of its strong evidence base, VIPP-SD is the only intervention that NICE recommends for pre-school children in its guidelines on attachment disorders

(2015): *Children's attachment: attachment in children and young people who are adopted from care, in care or at high risk of going into care.*

VIPP-SD can be funded via the Adoption Support Fund.

What is involved

VIPP-SD is usually carried out with the mother and child. This is because it is thought that involving both parents would complicate the process.

Practitioners are health or social care workers who have been trained to use this intervention. Most of them will be female, as they are working primarily with mothers. Their role is not to be a therapist or a teacher – it has been called an "intervener".

At each visit the practitioner makes short recordings of interactions between the mother and child as they play or interact together during daily routines. At the next session, the practitioner and the mother view the recording and discuss it together and the practitioner gives feedback, using the recording to show the mother what she is doing well and how she could develop her skills and sensitivity.

The sessions

The practitioner visits the mother at home for one to two hours per session. Each visit starts with a recording session of around 10 to 20 minutes, with the practitioner using a small hand-held video recorder. The practitioner studies the recording, following a protocol, and prepares comments and advice for the next home visit. After the recording session, the practitioner and the mother view and discuss the recordings from the previous visit together. The practitioner highlights examples of the mother's sensitivity, responsiveness, communication and strengths and acknowledges any positive changes in her behaviour or that of the child.

Phase 1 – the first two visits – focuses on the child's perspective, looking at exploration and attachment. The practitioner "speaks for the child", saying what they believe the child is conveying by his or her behaviour, and helps the mother to look at the child's behaviour in a different way.

In Phase 2 – visits 3 and 4 – the focus is on the way the mother deals with the child, looking at emotions and empathy. The practitioner shows her how positive parenting behaviour, such as praise, can be effective, and discusses strategies to deal sensitively with different situations, such as tantrums.

Phase 3 comprises booster sessions that look again at all the themes of previous visits.

The VIPP-SD intervention designed by the Centre for Child and Family Research at Leiden allows for four to six visits over four to six months but this may vary slightly in some programmes.

Nurturing Attachments

This group programme was developed by consultant clinical psychologist Dr Kim Golding who is a member of the board of directors for the Dyadic Developmental Psychotherapy Institute and also trains in DDP. Psychologists, social workers and other professionals involved in training adoptive parents use Golding's training resource to lead groups for adopters.

There are three modules, with six three-hour sessions per module:

- Module 1 provides an understanding of attachment theory, patterns of attachment and an introduction to therapeutic parenting.

- Module 2 provides guidance on how to help children experience their family as a secure base.

- Module 3 looks at how parents can both build a relationship with their children and manage their behaviour.

Groups contain a maximum of 15 parents.

SafeBase

The adoption support organisation After Adoption offers the four-day SafeBase Therapeutic Parenting Programme.

According to After Adoption, the programme aims to strengthen the relationships between parents and their children, improving the stability of the family. It includes the following topics:

- Putting attachment and child development into context for the family

- Explaining the impact of early adversity on brain development
- Explaining how early trauma impacts on a child's ability to develop security and trust
- Teaching practical techniques to build positive attachments with children and modify negative behaviour
- Helping parents create family stories to promote attachment and identity
- Enabling parents to exchange ideas and obtain mutual support.

The programme starts with a filmed structured play session at a venue near the family's home, with a follow-up feedback session looking at the child's strengths and difficulties. Then parents attend four days of training in therapeutic parenting. Afterwards there are regular support groups for parents.

SafeBase in the Teenage Years is a follow-up one-day course for parents who have already completed the SafeBase Therapeutic Parenting Programme. It was developed in response to SafeBase-trained parents who found they needed extra help when their children became teenagers. It helps parents to recognise the transitions their adolescent children are going through and the challenges they are facing, and it aims to help parents feel supported and reduce stress and family breakdown.

SafeBase has been in use for 15 years and, according to After Adoption, it is the most successful specialist therapeutic parenting programme for adoptive families in the UK, with many local authorities now offering the SafeBase programme to adoptive parents. After Adoption says it has proved to be effective for adoptive families for years after parents have attended the programme.
www.after-adoption.org.uk

Enhancing Adoptive Parenting

This is a programme to support adoptive parents in the early days to help them understand and manage difficult behaviour from their children. It was developed by Professors Alan Rushton and Elizabeth Monck and is offered by PAC-UK as a one-to-one training programme with parent(s) that can be conducted face-to-face or via Skype. Parents have 10 one-and-a-half hour sessions with a counsellor.

The topics covered include:

- Attachment

- How children develop new relationships

- Using positive attention to change behaviour

- The use of praise and rewards

- The use of clear commands and boundaries

- The use of ignoring

- Effective discipline, limit-setting and logical consequences

- Problem-solving with children.

Optional extra sessions cover a range of behaviours, including wetting and soiling, sexualised behaviour, difficulties in sibling and peer relationships, emotional and internal regulation, fears and anxieties and eating and sleeping problems.

PAC says that EAP has been tested for effectiveness in a randomised controlled trial as part of the Department for Education's Adoption Research Initiative (Rushton and Monck, 2009). The trial determined that the EAP programme was an effective aid to the parenting of abused and/or neglected children recently placed for adoption, with families demonstrating significantly positive change six months later, compared to a control group who had been given routine support.

www.pac-uk.org

Parenting our Children: Six steps to empowered parenting

This is Adoption UK's parenting programme. It's a six-day programme designed for up to 16 adoptive parents who have had children placed with them for at least six months. The training is delivered by experienced trainers who are also adoptive parents.

The six steps are:

- Expectations, realities and loss

- Child development, developmental trauma and recovery

- Claiming and belonging

- Trauma and adaptive behaviour

- Rewiring

- Developing positive self-esteem and sense of identity (this module also looks at contact with birth family members).
www.adoptionuk.org.uk

STOP

This is a 10-week parenting programme for parents of adopted children between 11 and 15 years old. It is offered by Coram as part of the agency's post-adoption support for its own adopters but other adopters can also attend.

It aims to help parents improve their relationship with their child or teenager and manage behaviour problems such as anger, controlling behaviour, poor social interaction with peers, difficulty expressing emotions and attachment issues.
www.coram.org.uk

Triple P

The Triple P programme or Positive Parenting Programme originated in Australia, where it was developed by Professor Matt Sanders and his colleagues from the Parenting and Family Support Centre at the University of Queensland.

It is not specifically designed for adoptive families. It aims to reduce "problem" behaviour in children by improving parents' understanding and their parenting skills and reducing stress in family life.

Triple P has over 20 different programmes and levels of training for parents of children at different ages and stages, from short talks and discussion groups on particular issues such as toddler tantrums, bedtimes, self-esteem and peer pressure to longer-term one-to-one support. There is an eight-week course consisting of four two-hour sessions followed by three weeks of telephone support and then a final session. There is a special training course for parents of children with a disability.

The Triple P programme has been in use since the 1970s and is now used in 25 countries worldwide. In the UK it is offered at some children's centres and

by some local authority children's services as well as by independent trained parent support practitioners.
www.triplep-parenting.uk.net

The Incredible Years (Webster-Stratton) Parenting Programme

This parenting course was developed over 30 years ago by Professor Carolyn Webster-Stratton, Director of the Parenting Clinic, University of Washington, USA. It is now in extensive use in Canada, Australia, New Zealand, the US, Russia and several EU countries including England. It is aimed at parents of children with conduct disorders or behavioural problems, and groups of parents meet for two-hour sessions for 10 to 12 weeks. The programme now includes a number of different training packages for parents of children in different age groups, as well as classroom management programmes for teachers. Others have since built on the original programme, adapting the material for use with adoptive parents and specifically addressing issues around adopted children.

The basic elements include:

- Using play to build relationships

- Using praise, positive attention and rewards

- Setting limits and boundaries

- Consequences for misbehaviour

- Problem-solving and anger management.

In the UK the original Incredible Years programme is offered by some children's centres, children's services and schools, usually for parents of children from the age of two to eight or nine. Some adoption agencies and support organisations offer the Incredible Years Adoptive Parenting Programme.
www.incredibleyears.com (the US website)

Adopting Together – Relationship support for adoptive parents

The Tavistock Centre for Couple Relationships (TCCR) is offering free, Government-funded support for adoptive couples. It has created this specialised service to respond to the needs of adoptive couples who wish to explore and strengthen their relationship following adoption. The Adopting Together Service is open to all post-adoption parents (also for couples where the children have been placed but not yet adopted and for Special Guardians) and both heterosexual and same-sex couples can be seen in either couples therapy or parent groups.

Working with experienced therapists, couples can get help and support to address some of the issues that are impacting on their relationship. The specialist services can help by:

- Offering a safe space to reflect on how adoption has impacted on the couple relationship

- Allowing for better communication between couples

- Supporting couples with difficulties they may be experiencing

- Improving the quality of the relationship

After attending a consultation appointment, couples may be offered the Adopting Together Therapeutic Groups.
www.tccr.org.uk/adopting-together

INTERVENTIONS FOR YOUNG PEOPLE WHOSE BEHAVIOUR IS CHALLENGING AND/OR VIOLENT

The teenage years can be stressful for many families and that includes those with adopted children. In a small but significant number of adoptive families, this stress can be sincere and result from a wide range of issues. This might include severe depression and/or anxiety, eating disorders, problems at school or with friends, inappropriate sexual behaviour and the use of drugs and alcohol. Although not a new phenomenon, child-to-parent violence has come to be recognised as one aspect of this for some families, with a young person's threats, intimidation, aggression and violence against parents and/or other children in the family causing a great deal of stress and suffering.

The focus on providing help to families during the teenage years has significantly increased in both youth justice and social work services. The specific focus on child-to-parent violence was identified as a key factor in many adoption disruptions in Julie Selwyn's research *Beyond the Adoption Order* (2015). Professor Selwyn and colleagues pointed out that all too frequently the response from services was to blame the adoptive parents and to instigate child protection investigations. She identified an urgent need for professionals to recognise child-to-parent violence and develop evaluated interventions.

Multi-systemic therapy

Multi-systemic therapy (MST) is an intensive intervention for young people aged 11 to 17 whose severe behaviour problems may include offending, putting them at greater risk of an out-of-home or custodial placement.

Core principles

The aim is to keep the young person at home, in school or college and out of trouble by providing intensive support to bring about lasting positive changes in behaviour.

Therapy is home- and community-based. It involves the whole family as well as the young person's school, friends and other people they may be involved with. Parents are key to working with the therapist.

Therapists look at the young person's and family's strengths and how to build on these, as well as looking at the young person's problems and how these "fit" with the broader context of his life, family, friends and so on. The emphasis is on the present and the future, rather than on gaining insight about the reasons or looking into the past.

An MST team consists of a supervisor, three or four MST therapists, an administrator and a part-time back-up supervisor. MST therapists are, for example, psychologists, family therapists, senior social workers, mental health nurses or probation officers with experience of working with children and families in a community setting, who have attended a five-day training course organised by MST-UK. Supervisors have additional training. Training is only available to people working in a licensed MST treatment programme.

In some locations, MST services also offer adaptations to the standard MST programme to address problematic sexual behaviour, substance abuse and other issues.

History

MST was developed in the 1980s in the US at the Family Services Research Centre of the Department of Psychiatry and Behavioural Sciences, Medical University of South Carolina. The aim was to improve mental health services for young people in trouble with the law.

In 1996, a private for-profit corporation called MST Services was formed to disseminate the method, to train new MST teams, and provide supervision for therapists. At the same time, a non-profit organisation called the MST Institute was formed, to be responsible for ensuring that the implementation of MST worldwide met the right standards.

As well as MST teams in the US and the rest of Europe, there are now 35 teams in England, Scotland and Northern Ireland (and more teams are being set up). MST-UK is a partner of MST Services in the US. It is a public sector service that supports and trains people working in MST teams and ensures that MST services follow the MST model properly.

What the therapy involves

MST includes elements of family therapy and cognitive behaviour therapy (see p32).

Treatment is individualised. Together with the parents, the therapist will devise a treatment plan targeting the problems and setting goals for the young person to meet (such as coming home on time, attending school and so on). The therapist will work with the parents, helping them with problem-solving and strategies to use to encourage positive change.

The idea is that one therapist focuses on the family, rather than having several different professionals involved. Therapists generally work with just four to six families at a time and are on call 24/7 to deal with crises. They receive weekly guidance and feedback about their work with families.

Some MST teams offer a special adaptation of MST for young people who abuse substances. In these cases, the therapist looks at the underlying factors, helps produce a written plan for parents to enforce – with random drugs tests, incentives and consequences for their child – and trains the young person in how to refuse drugs (e.g. role-playing).

The sessions

MST therapists meet frequently with the family and the young person and this happens at the family home rather than a clinic. The therapist is also likely to go to the young person's school or spend time with his or her friends and extended family members in order to get a good idea of what is going on and what factors are contributing to the young person's problems.

There may be several visits a week from the therapist at first, and visits will decrease as the treatment programme goes on.

The support given is intensive over a period of three to five months, with the aim of empowering the family to continue with the strategies and interventions that were successful.

Non-violent resistance (NVR)

Parents, including adoptive parents, who are being intimidated, controlled and even frequently hit, punched or kicked by their child are understandably desperate and distressed but often struggle to access the right kind of help. Social workers may be at a loss as to what to suggest. The kind of therapies and therapeutic parenting programmes outlined above may simply not be enough when a young person's behaviour is so extreme – and in any case many troubled young people refuse to attend therapy. Non-violent resistance is a specific programme for parents that provides a strategy to deal with threatening behaviour and violence from a child towards them or other family members and to bring about a more peaceful and harmonious atmosphere in the family.

Core principles

When a child is violent and aggressive, parents often use a strategy that attempts to control the child's behaviour but most children respond by refusing to be controlled. This results in an escalation of the behaviour from the child and an escalation of the attempt to control by the parents. So the confrontation continues to intensify. Parents can end up feeling helpless or as though they are "walking on eggshells". Non-violent resistance recognises that escalation is not an effective way of dealing with such threatening situations, and alternative methods of communication need to be developed that clearly indicate that the violence is not acceptable but within a strategy that de-

3

escalates the behaviour and provides a positive solution to the issues that drive the behaviour.

History

"Non-violent resistance" (NVR) was developed as a parent training programme by Haim Omer, Professor of Psychology at Tel Aviv University in Israel. It was based on the principle of peaceful protest aimed at overcoming injustice, such as the civil rights movement. It was introduced to the UK in 2006 by Dr Peter Jakob, a clinical psychologist who developed it for use with looked after children and traumatised, multi-stressed families. Dr Jakob, now Director of Consultancy at PartnershipProjects, has since trained a number of family therapists, clinical psychologists and other mental health professionals in how to deliver this intervention through CAMHS or in other settings.

What the therapy involves

Parents are taught strategies for use at home with their child, which relate to the key elements of the NVR programme:

- Making a stand against the young person's violent behaviour by communicating their intention to resist it without using physical or verbal aggression

- Ensuring wherever possible that there is no escalation in the interaction between the child and parents

- Protecting the victims (e.g. themselves or a sibling)

- Enlisting the help of friends and relatives who can act as mediators and supporters – trusted people who know the child, who can provide support to the parents, act as "witnesses" so that the child knows that what's going on isn't being kept secret, and step in to defuse explosive situations when necessary

- Using increased "parental presence" to change the child's behaviour – this may be in the form of a "sit-in" in the child's room after a major incident, until the child makes a constructive proposal

- Taking steps towards reconciliation with the child, such as messages of respect and appreciation and suggestions of joint activities.

The sessions

NVR can be delivered as a course of therapy for a family – with some sessions in the agency and others with the therapist going to their home – or as a group programme for a number of parents together. Some adoption support agencies offer one-day workshops to serve as an introduction to NVR methods, but this is not the same as having the actual therapeutic intervention. When NVR is given as an intensive intervention, it can last for three to four months or longer if necessary. Parents are taught and supported to use the approach by a clinical psychologist or other therapist over 12 weekly sessions, with "homework" – strategies to try at home – and telephone support between sessions. As well as the strategies above, parents are coached in how to avoid arguments, withstand provocation, stay calm and persevere.

Other family members or friends might also attend sessions to learn how they can become involved in the programme and offer support.

Break4Change

Break4Change is a programme developed for young people between 10 and 17 years old who exhibit abusive or violent behaviour to parents or carers. It is not specifically designed for adopted young people and is not yet widely available.

Core principles

Break4Change involves both the young person and their parents, working in parallel sessions. It aims to reduce violent behaviour in young people by changing values, beliefs and actions by improving their internal control, offering workable alternative strategies, increasing critical reasoning and enhancing empathy.

History

Break4Change was developed in Brighton and Hove in 2009, when workers were encountering families struggling with abusive young people who were behaving aggressively in their families and realised that there was no specific intervention to help them. Several professionals across a number of agencies working with young people – including youth crime prevention workers and family workers – co-operated to produce and pilot a training programme.

What the programme involves

There are two parallel groups, one for parents, the other for young people, running for 12 weeks. Agnes Munday from Rise, one of the organisations involved in developing and evaluating the programme, wrote that the aims of Break4Change include:

- Reduce parents' feelings of isolation and young people's feelings of entitlement

- Challenge parents' feelings of guilt and deterministic thinking about causes (e.g. 'he/she can't help it because of ADHD' or 'his/her father was violent')

- Create a realistic belief in the possibility of change

- Clarify boundaries of what is acceptable and unacceptable behaviour and balance entitlement with responsibilities

- Help parents develop strategies for creating meaningful consequences for unacceptable behaviour

- Reinforce each progressive step and provide emotional support for adults as they attempt to become more assertive in their parenting and for young people while they focus on finding non-abusive solutions to problems

- Explore anger (the child's and the parents')

- Help parents to feel less depressed and powerless, and decrease the incidence of violent and abusive behaviour in the family.

The sessions

The 12 two-hour sessions for the young person and their parents involve a mixture of presentations, interactive exercises and discussion. The young people's sessions also have a creative element.

Parents' sessions cover subjects such as understanding teenagers' development and behaviour, relationships, goal-setting, parenting styles, strategies for managing behaviour (including drugs, alcohol and sex) and encouraging positive behaviour, the management of angry feelings, and how to be appropriately assertive. They also cover the need for parents to care for themselves.

The sessions for young people encourage them to consider the feelings or situations that trigger angry feelings and violent behaviour, their own values and beliefs, and their goals for the future. This includes exploring ways of

Catchpoint

encouraging discovering celebrating becoming family

Catchpoint Consultancy CIC, founded in 2001, is a team of therapists and consultants who specialise in supporting families caring for children affected by developmental and complex trauma. We have combined creative arts and play therapies with current research in trauma recovery and attachment theory to offer **Creative Therapy and Support Programmes** with the aim of creating stability and security for troubled families. We work with:

- Children and Young People
- Adoptive Parents
- Foster Carers
- Kinship Carers
- Special Guardians
- Step Parents
- Residential Care Staff
- School Staff

We aim to set up a working partnership with parents or guardians, and include them in the therapy sessions.

Contact us at:
Catchpoint
Vassall Centre, Gill Avenue
Bristol BS16 2QQ
08450 944541
info@catchpoint.org
www.catchpoint.org

Catchpoint Team offer:

Expertise, experience and flexibility in working with traumatised children and their families, support teams, school staff and mentors
FREE initial consultation
Collaborative Assessment
Court Reports
Flexible Therapeutic Programmes including:

- Creative Arts and Play Therapy
- Life Story work
- Circle of Support meetings
- Parent/Carer/Guardian Support
- Whole Family sessions
- Attendance at Review meetings
- Short term intensive programme

Family Days
Family support through mentoring
Preparation for moving placement
Training and consultations for:

- Parents and carers
- Education staff
- Child Care professionals

SECTION 4
Finding a therapist who is right for your child

Choosing a therapist

If your child is assessed for support and the plan is to access the Adoption Support Fund, the adoption social worker or specialist carrying out the assessment will suggest suitable types of therapy and they may also propose approaching organisations or individual therapists that the local authority has worked with before. Above all, it is your child's needs and the issues that have been identified in the assessment that should determine which organisation or therapist is approached, with a clear sense of what the identified outcomes from the therapy are expected to be.

Through the assessment you should discuss and have some input into the choice of therapeutic approach and therapist – you know your child. And in many situations, it will be important to explore your child's thoughts and feelings about therapy and therapists in a way that is helpful to them. They need to be an important part of this process.

As the assessment and plans progress, it may be helpful for you to speak to the therapist or therapy organisation. You may have questions that they will be able to answer and help you to develop your view that the assessment has identified the right issues and the right approaches to working with those issues. Choosing a therapist who will be able to relate well to your child (and to whom your child will be able to relate) is important because the relationship that develops between them is key to achieving a good outcome.

How do you know if a therapist is properly trained, competent and trustworthy?

There is a bewildering array of professional bodies, accreditation schemes and approved registers for therapeutic approaches and providers of therapy. These professional bodies set standards for professional conduct and members are bound by an ethical framework for good practice.

Ofsted

Adoption support services or individual practitioners must be registered with Ofsted (unless they are part of the NHS), and an adoption support service or independent practitioner providing adoption support can be registered with Ofsted only if they meet certain minimum standards. However, when an independent practitioner is sub-contracted by a local authority to provide services for its adopters, the practitioner must be approved to practise by that local authority even if he or she does not have Ofsted registration of their own.

Health and Care Professions Council (HCPC)

The HCPC is a UK-wide health and care regulator set up to protect the public. It covers social workers in England and certain kinds of therapists, across the UK. It holds a register of health and care professionals who meet its standards of proficiency and who agree to be bound by their standards of conduct, performance and ethics. It regulates (among other professions) art therapists, occupational therapists, physiotherapists, practitioner psychologists, social workers in England, and speech and language therapists.

All of these professions have at least one professional title that is protected by law. This means that anyone using the title "art therapist" or "physiotherapist", for example, must be registered with the HCPC. It is a criminal offence for someone to use a protected title that they are not entitled to use.

However, it is important to note that the term "psychotherapist" is *not* a protected title.
www.hcpc-uk.org.uk

4

Professional bodies for therapists

Most therapists also belong to their own registration body. This means that they have met the requirements of that registration body regarding their training and the standards they observe as part of their practice. But registration bodies are not comparable and their training requirements and standards can vary a great deal from one organisation to another. Some require an extensive period of training over months or years, while a few can simply involve attending courses lasting several days. You can usually find out what's involved in the training in a particular therapy or therapeutic approach, and what accreditation from an organisation actually means, by discussing this with your social worker during assessment or exploring this yourself online.

> ...it is good practice for therapists to register with, or become "accredited" by, one of the organisations that set and monitor the standards expected of someone carrying out a particular type of therapy. It is important to note here that registration or accreditation of a particular organisation isn't the same level of involvement as membership.
>
> Registration/accreditation typically involves the presentation of evidence of training, competence and supervision that is examined in detail before being approved. Membership is open to a broader range of interested people who may not have had any training or assessment of competence but who may be bound by some of the guidelines for good practice of that organisation.

www.supportingsafetherapy.org
University of Sheffield Centre for Psychological Research

Professional bodies and contact information

Most of the therapies below require people to have a degree in teaching, social care or mental health as well as experience of working with children before studying for a postgraduate qualification.

Art therapy

Art therapists must have an MA or MSc in art therapy in order to legally practise as an art therapist or art psychotherapist in the UK. They must have completed a course of training validated by the HCPC.

Their professional body is the British Association of Art Therapists.
www.baat.org

Drama therapy

Dramatherapists are also registered with the HCPC.

British Association of Dramatherapists
www.badth.org.uk

Dialectical behaviour therapy

www.dbt-training.co.uk
www.behaviouraltech.org

Equine-assisted therapy and learning

www.eagala.org/UK
www.equineassistedqualifications.com

Filial therapy

There is a limited number of therapists trained and certified to carry out filial therapy in the UK. There is no central professional organisation for filial therapists in the UK. The following websites – websites of filial therapy practitioners who offer filial therapy and train professionals in using it – will tell you more about what's involved:

www.filialplaytherapy.co.uk (website of Geraldine Thomas)
www.filialtherapy.co.uk (website of Nina Rye)
www.playandfilialtherapy.co.uk (website of Virginia Ryan)

There is also some information about filial play on the website of Play Therapy UK but the organisation says that its preferred approach is to provide coaching/mentoring for parents in nurturing skills and how to play non-directively with their children.

Family therapy

Association for Family Therapy
www.aft.org.uk

4

Multi-systemic therapy

www.mstuk.org

Music therapy

Music therapists must have done an approved course and be registered with the HCPC in order to use the title "music therapist".

Their professional body is the British Association for Music Therapy.
www.bamt.org

Play therapy

British Association of Play Therapists
www.bapt.info

Play Therapy UK – the UK Society for Play and Creative Arts Therapies
www.playtherapy.org.uk

Psychotherapy

The title "psychotherapist" is not protected by law. But some variations of the title, e.g. "registered psychotherapist", indicate a high level of training.

There are a number of professional bodies for psychotherapists. Each professional body differs in their requirements for membership and/or accreditation. For example, a psychotherapist might be registered with the British Association for Counselling and Psychotherapy (the largest and broadest body with over 41,000 members), or the UK Council for Psychotherapy or the Association of Child and Adolescent Psychotherapists.

The registers of the professional bodies below are themselves certified by the Professional Standards Authority for Health and Social Care, which independently assesses organisations that hold registers of practitioners.

- Association of Child and Adolescent Psychotherapists
  www.childpsychotherapy.org.uk

- British Association for Counselling and Psychotherapy
  www.bacp.org.uk

- UK Council for Psychotherapy
  www.psychotherapy.org.uk

- British Association for Behavioural and Cognitive Psychotherapies
  www.babcp.com
- Association for Family Therapy and Systemic Practice
  www.aft.org.uk

Sensory processing therapy

Sensory Integration Network
www.sensoryintegration.org.uk

Theraplay

Theraplay UK is an affiliate of the Theraplay Institute, which sets international standards for Theraplay treatment and training. Only those who have been certified by the Theraplay Institute can describe themselves as Theraplay therapists.
www.theraplay.org.uk

Some questions to ask yourself and/or the therapist

You want to find the right therapist as well as the right therapy. Don't be afraid to ask questions.

- What type or types of therapy does the therapist use?
- Are they adoption-experienced and knowledgeable?
- What is he/she aiming to achieve for your child and/or your family?
- Can he/she explain to your satisfaction how the therapy works?
- How many sessions are there likely to be (some therapies are open-ended)?
- Has the therapist had experience and training with children and young people who have experienced trauma? What kind of training was it and how long has he/she been doing this type of work? Is he/she qualified and certified by the appropriate professional body or organisation? Does he/she have regular supervision by an experienced clinical supervisor?
- Is the therapist's personal style empowering for you as a parent? Does he/she seem calm, open and honest? Is he/she happy to answer your

questions? Does he/she give a sense that they understand what life is like for you and your child?

● Will you be involved at all with your child's therapy? If not, will the therapist meet with you on a regular basis to discuss how the therapy with your child is progressing and your thoughts and feelings about this?

4

Working with a therapist: potential drawbacks and difficulties

It's easy to see how therapies might improve things for your child and for your family. But there can be complications and it is important to recognise these.

Research carried out at the University of Sheffield Centre for Psychological Services Research was funded by the UK National Institute for Health Research to look at understanding and preventing adverse effects of psychological therapies. The website **www.supportingsafetherapy.org** is based on the researchers' findings.

They did not look specifically at adoption support therapies or therapies for children and young people. However, they do say the following:

> *Most people do find therapy helpful and it has been shown to be an effective treatment for a range of mental health problems. However, some people have a bad experience of therapy and their mental health gets worse, not better. Sometimes people can be harmed by therapy, just as there are sometimes negative effects from medication.*

Equally, there are some therapies where the child's problems may actually appear to get worse, especially at the beginning of the process where anxieties can be stirred up – an unknown person in an unknown setting exploring difficult issues especially where the fear of blame and humiliation may play a part. Where recalling and exploring memories of neglect, abuse or loss are also a part of therapy, this places important responsibilities on the therapist in terms of sensitivity, empathy and the support and reassurance they provide. The developing relationships between the child, the parents and the therapist are key to this and persevering through the initial period of "getting to know you" is essential.

Arranging therapy for a child can also evoke anxious feelings for adoptive parents. They might be worried that the therapist will blame them for poor parenting – not having the right parenting skills or having the wrong expectations of the child. They might have to explore the child's past in new ways and discover upsetting experiences along the way. They may also have experienced the "secondary trauma" that can result from caring for a child who has been traumatised by abuse and neglect. Parents need access to their own support and this needs to be appropriately identified in the assessment. This might be provided by therapy or counselling for themselves or something directly linked to the child's therapy.

There are other potential issues associated with therapy. You might feel that if your child is having therapy it will "label" him and make him feel different from his peers. This might also be an issue for the child with their friends or at school – stigma, name calling or bullying.

Any therapeutic work can be quite demanding for families and can take a lot of work. Different therapies make different demands on time, resources and energy and this must be built into the plan. These issues need to be talked about and support provided.

If it's not working out

If you are not happy with the therapist or the therapy or you are worried about the effect it is having on your child, you (and your child) are not obliged to continue. It is not your job to keep the therapist happy. But if this is the case, speak to the therapist about the problems or difficulties and try to work them out. You could also discuss the issues with your social worker to see what experiences and thoughts they might have.

If you want to make a complaint about a therapist, you would normally complain to the therapist's employer in the first instance (e.g. the NHS, the local authority or the adoption support agency). You could also complain to the therapist's professional or registration body. If you are concerned that there are any safeguarding issues in respect of your child, then you must raise these with an appropriate professional as a matter of urgency.

SECTION 5
Personal accounts

Below we reproduce some blogs and/or extracts from blogs written by adoptive parents and an adopted teenager in which they describe therapeutic interventions and approaches and support groups that they have found helpful.

Dr Bruce Perry speaks at the Adoption UK conference 2014

By Sally Donovan

www.sallydonovan.co.uk/2014/11/16/drbruceperry/

Frankly I get pissed off with being told that developmental trauma isn't a real thing. Yesterday 250 people who live with the everyday realities of trauma in children gathered for the Adoption UK 2014 conference to listen to Dr Bruce Perry speak. Not once were we told to put more structure in place, or to set up a system of rewards and sanctions, or to lecture more or to just pull ourselves together and grow some backbone.

It became clear to me quite early on that I was sharing my life with two children who see threat everywhere. They see it in eye contact, tone of voice, they smell it in certain smells, they expect it to result from the most benign of circumstances. There is not a single week, or day, or hour or sometimes minute when I am not reminded that their inner working models are based around threat and the expectation that others are not well-intentioned. I'm told that there is little scientific evidence for all this. To that my response is, come and live in my house for a couple of weeks.

Now that's off my chest, here are a few of the most relevant things I learnt or was reminded of yesterday:

1. The brain develops templates based on experience. If its template for "person who I live with" is lack of care/hurt/fear then this is what it will expect of future

"person who I live with" (or who teaches me or otherwise tries to care for me or who tells me to do stuff). This is why I get accused of shouting, being threatening and hating everyone if I ask someone to take the rubbish out or brush their teeth.

2. Shifting these templates takes consistency, permanency and persistence. This is why I always feel I am fighting the templates ('You are SHOUTING at me'/'I'm talking in a normal voice, see how quiet it is'/'STOP SHOUTING'/'I'm not shouting'/'Yes you are, I hate you, you child abuser').

3. The brain at first sees novelty as a threat ('Would you like to watch this programme with me about space?'/'No, get lost, I hate you'/'Shall I take that as a no then?'/'Fuck off').

4. Our children are sensitised to threat. (This is so obvious I can't understand why it's not accepted.)

5. Children respond to stresses by fight, flight or dissociation. I live with one of each, but both can use either, depending...They dysregulate easily (again, so obvious).

6. A dysregulated child needs the support of a regulated adult. We have to act as their external regulatory system. A dysregulated adult cannot hope to help regulate a child. Ever.

7. Self-care is the most important part of therapeutic parenting/teaching, etc.

8. Rhythm calms dysregulated children; music (listening and playing), walking, cycling, bouncing, talking, car journeys.

9. Take a step back from a dysregulated child and lower your voice (reduce the perception of threat).

10. Reward schemes are constructed with the assumption that children are choosing to be aggressive/fidgety/chatty/gobby. They are not. They are dysregulated and therefore not operating in the thinking part of their brains.

11. Children with poor templates around relationships need lots of space around them. Try standing or sitting parallel to them. This is why one of my children talks and talks and shares loads every evening that I drive him to his club. Then he falls asleep (that's the rhythmic thing about engines). This could also be why children flip out at school when adults flood in around them at times of stress (again, obvious?).

12. Children need regular time to dissociate, i.e. veg out. For us this is particularly noticeable after school. Don't hit them with 'How was your day?', or 'Do you have any homework?' Give space and time and then go in gently (regulate then connect).

But what does this all mean practically? In our family, it means playing music at mealtimes, making more time to massage each others' shoulders and generally being a bit more mindful of trying to keep regulated, whilst all the while remembering that it's not possible to get it right all the time.

© Sally Donovan[1]

Blog on DDP (among other things)

Saturday 21 November 2015

http://journeythroughadoption.blogspot.co.uk/2015/11/living-with-attachment

disorder.html

Living with Attachment Disorder

Perhaps the best support we've had is that G and I have been referred to a DDP Family Therapist. This is someone that specialises in families with attachment challenges. G and I see her most weeks, and whilst it's not an overnight fix, what it has done is given us both space to explore our feelings and to debrief on Charlie's weekly activities, and really start to stand back and think about what's going on in that little body of his.

It's slowly enabling us to move on from our anger and frustration, to start reconnecting with why he acts like he does. It's helped me to rediscover my empathy and to think about what his behaviour is telling us. It's reminding us that the behaviour is an outward expression of an underlying cause, and instead of dealing with the behaviour (the symptom), we need to fix the underlying cause. And what's become clear, is there's still a lot of hurt and insecurity in that little guy.

---

1   Sally Donovan is a member of the Adoption Support Expert Advisory Group, a group of Adoption Champions that was set up in October 2015 to advise and challenge ministers on how to improve help and support for adoptive families.

5

So, for example, in our first session I talked about my frustration in the fact that even the most basic rules, the ones we repeat daily, are still broken daily. G often describes it as a sense of "groundhog day" with him, where you just feel like you're making no progress. Sarah, our DDP therapist, talked to us about "connect before correct", that is to say, that there's no point correcting his behaviour until you've really connected with him in the moment. Because in his aroused state – his brain chemicals are in self-preservation mode (like fight or flight) – there's no capacity to listen to the parental lecture that's about to happen. So, later that same day the four of us were at home. I was upstairs, Joe was in the dining room doing his homework, Charlie was playing in his room and G shouted up that he was just nipping out to the corner shop for some bread. I heard G leave, I then heard Charlie run downstairs and open the front door. Charlie has no sense of danger, so we have strict rules around not opening the front door. The previous day I wold have marched downstairs and given him a dressing down for opening the front door when he knows the family rule about that. But armed with the DDP session we had just come from, instead I went down, knelt down next to Charlie and hugged him, and I whispered in his ear 'Oh Charlie, my job is to keep you safe, and I want to do that more than anything in the world. That's why we don't want you to open the front door when Daddy and Papa aren't here, just in case it's a stranger on the other side of the door.' Instead of the stand-off that I would normally have expected in this situation, Charlie burst into tears and said, 'I don't know where Papa's gone. Will he ever come home?'

So there it was right there, the underlying insecurity in Charlie. Despite everything, Charlie knows that adults aren't actually all that reliable. Sometimes the people he's loved the most (birth parents, foster carers) have let him down, they've not been there, and who's to say that no matter how good life might be on the surface right now, G and I won't prove ourselves to be just as unreliable as the last adults that he had learned to love. Charlie is still a little boy with a lot of hurt inside.

And of course, had I been cross, I would never have heard that.

So, whilst we're still in this crazy life, we've now started to understand him so much more. And just admitting that Charlie has special needs has helped us to start to unpick both his behaviours and our own. And that feels so much more positive than it felt four months ago.

Resilience: loving a child with Foetal Alcohol Spectrum Disorder

By FASD Mum

https://fasdlearningwithhope.wordpress.com/2015/09/27/resilience/

My husband and I spent four hours at an FASD support group yesterday. About three of those hours were spent slowly taking turns around the room, hearing and discussing each other's stories. Learning about the children each person loved and how prenatal exposure to alcohol has affected them. It was a positive environment, skillfully led, with input from some experts who were also there, experts who have also raised kids with FASD. It was a room full of hope and determination.

I was nervous before we went. I developed a new appreciation for the courage of those who attend Alcoholics Anonymous and other support groups. It is not easy to come forward and to say you or your family need help, that you can't do it alone, that you need support. I have always failed those trust tests where you are supposed to fall back and let others catch you. I didn't know what to expect. I didn't want to hear more bad news.

What I heard, as we went around that room, slowly and respectfully sharing our experiences, was that we are not alone. There are others out there, who know and who understand. But it was more than that. I know the statistics. We are connected with many really helpful support networks in cyberspace. Social media is a gift. It has helped us immensely to be in touch with families, experts, adults with FASD. But there in that peaceful room we were able to look into each others' eyes, to see the pain, the fear, the rugged determination, the will to fight shining through the frustration and tears. It was humbling but uplifting.

And yes, as I had dreaded, it was also a room that held some of my worst nightmares – those things you fear for your child when you lay awake, trying to suppress the panic. The vulnerability of our kids laid bare. Prison. Sexual violence. Isolation. Ostracism. Self-harm. Rejection. And yet, there it was – the mind-blowing and inspiring resilience of people whose loved ones have suffered through those worst things of all. They were saying, 'We're still here, we're still fighting, and look! Our kids are not only progressing, they are doing well.' You can come through even great darkness to the other side. I never thought to face down those fears.

5

There were three birth mums in the room. Their power and their presence smoothed the anger I realised I had been harbouring toward our son's birth mother. It's a whole other level of bravery to stare down the stigma, to put your child's wellbeing ahead of your own defensiveness and fight like hell for your kids.

There was an intergenerational nature to the meeting that was refreshing. There were parents and relatives of young people ranging from toddlers to the late 20s. We were recognising our own experiences in others with kids of similar ages. We were learning from those with older kids and maybe even helping those with younger children. We learned more about legal structures that can help. We heard of best practices for educating professionals. We discussed ways to interact with schools to create more positive learning environments. We saw selfless volunteerism in action. We heard about endless hours some have spent trying to widen the services available to families affected by FASD. It was a lot to take in. Honestly, I felt exhausted when I left. I just needed it to sink in. I wasn't sure what it all meant.

But then, this. This morning I told our son that we met many families yesterday who had children with FASD. He said, still trying to comprehend our various, gentle conversations about this over months, 'Do I have FASD?' I said, 'Yes, you do. And yesterday we heard about some amazing things that kids with FASD have done when they have grown up. And we heard more about other kids with FASD, kids who get frustrated, kids who forget things. You are not alone. But you know what? As you grow up, you'll figure things out. You'll learn how to manage things so you don't always feel like this. We'll help you.' And as I said it, I realised I had more confidence in these words, words that I have said before. He will absorb that confidence as together we walk on into his tomorrows.

© fasdLearningWithHope

Finding support:
The group we attended was organised by NOFAS UK. They can be contacted via a helpline at 020 8458 5951.

The FASD Trust also sponsors support groups. Their helpline is 01608 811599.

There are similar groups in a wide range of countries – when in doubt, Google!

Bruce Perry: my top ten takeaways

By Mo and Bro

https://moandbro.wordpress.com/

Yesterday, along with lots of other fabulous folk, we heard Bruce Perry speak on 'The effects of trauma and neglect on childhood development' at Adoption UK's 2014 conference in Birmingham.

With neurons and neural networks aplenty, there was lots to take in. And as well as loads of factoids about brains, Bruce (no surname required, you know, like a celebrity) brought humour to the day. Made us laugh. Always a good thing.

Anyhow, my top 10 takeaways from the day:

1   Get up 10 mins earlier – give yourself half a chance of everyone starting the day regulated.

2   Intimacy overwhelms our children (yet we crave it).

3   Negative feedback, from anyone about anything, makes our children feel dysregulated (course it does).

4   When it comes to child brain development, essentially, all models are wrong… but some are useful.

5   We're not just parents, we're external regulators: Regulate, Relate, Reason (we have to Connect before we can Correct).

6   Rhythm is the way to regulate kids. And adults. Rocking desks…

7   Most important to take care of ourselves: we need a self-care strategy for our entire day.

8   When all hell breaks loose: be present, be parallel, let them control, lower your voice and move away.

9   Walking is great for regulating, as is making and listening to music. Riding bikes, watching TV, playing video games all good after-school regulators too. (Note to self: time to get a dog.)

10 Some children are hyper-aroused, some dissociate, some do both. The brain's way of coping with trauma.

One thing's for sure, brains are really, really cool.

Dan Hughes: my top ten takeaways

Today I heard Dan Hughes, clinical psychologist, speak: The Place for Parenting, at Adoption UK's Belfast conference.

5

Many have heard Dan speak before and all say they take away something new each time. I can see why – he' s a great storyteller, clever and funny. A mixed crowd in Belfast today: prospective adopters, adoptive parents, practitioners and teachers (note to self to speak to school). T'was a good day and I have a lot to ponder.

In the meantime, my top 10 takeaways from the day:

1   The dummy is OK – no need to fuss, what's an orthodontist's bill compared to our child's emotional well-being?

2   When she grunts or growls (or both!) don't say 'Use your words' – she can't muster the words so don't shame her.

3   Never watch *Super Nanny* ever again.

4   Really understand her wobbly sense of self (and mine sometimes).

5   When she won't cuddle, show her how I'll cuddle her in my mind – even if she thinks I'm weird!

6   When I don't feel like having fun, fake it (it will come).

7   No judgement, no annoyance, just curiosity about how she feels.

8   Don't even think about Disneyland: traumatised, brain fried...

9   PACE (for birth child Big Bro too) Playfulness, Acceptance, Curiosity, Empathy.

10 Look after mums too.

Tired now, brain fried, looking forward to getting home. For a cuddle.

© Mo and Bro

Mo and Bro: An adoption blog by two mums, who have a birth son and an adopted daughter

An adopted teenager writes…

www.at-id.org.uk/our-stories/

There it was out of the blue at one in the morning, a message on Facebook saying 'Hiya! I'm your birth mum and I'm always here for you.'

I've always known my life story and even meet my birth nana and auntie every year but what was I going to do? I was a typical 15-year-old with my head full of stuff about dyeing my hair, prom dresses and what to do with the rest of my life but wasn't prepared for this!

I told my parents after a couple of days and they went ballistic but it kind of ended up being my fault for some reason. I hadn't done anything wrong and just didn't know where to turn. My friends at school didn't understand adoption stuff (and I didn't advertise it anyway) and no teenager wants to talk about big stuff with their mum and dad – no way!

Soon after, I got a post on Facebook from some bloke saying he was my natural father and introducing me to my "brothers and sisters". I was really angry. How dare they just barge into my world. I hadn't asked for this and it just all felt out of control.

Anyway, the police got involved and it got sorted out and I get the odd random post now but nothing more. It really played on my mind and messed with my head though. I felt completely alone and got really depressed and just didn't know what to do.

I went to see a counsellor and that helped a lot...just someone who listens but doesn't judge you, where you can say what you like without worrying about offending anyone. Someone who is not involved and doesn't take sides...I also got a lot of support by meeting up with other adopted teenagers and realising that I wasn't on my own and this made me feel less different and more confident in just getting on with things.

I'm 18 now and just got good A-level results and my future is bright!! Some of this stuff has been a real challenge but I've got through it and come out the other end, wiser and stronger.

It's normal when you are a teenager to try to figure out who you are but this stuff runs much deeper if you're adopted, because it's messier and complicated to get your head around.

Treading on eggshells

By Mending Mum

Friday 22 May 2015

http://mrsowpa.blogspot.co.uk/

I used to work as an adviser on safeguarding! I never believed I would become at risk myself from my own child. I became more vulnerable as she became bigger and more controlling, I also had a long-term medical condition that made me tired and wobbly and off balance at times.

Anger or "red mist" has always been an issue, but became worse when she got to 11. Unfortunately she becomes angry very quickly and finds it difficult to recognise the signs and try to calm herself down. Her angry response would normally be vile, hateful language and throwing the nearest thing to hand. The thrown object could be something she cared about, like a phone, and at someone she cared about, like us, but in that red mist moment logical thinking does not happen. Kicking, pushing, slapping and gripping arms until they hurt and bruised were also common.

The most common triggers for the red mist are being told "no", things not going to plan or confiscation of an electronic device. However, the reaction does depend slightly on how she is doing at school, what friends she has and how happy or not she is generally with life.

Over the last couple of years, she is now nearly 15, we have had support from CAMHS, an adoption support social worker and another family therapist. We have also attended SafeBase training and post-adoption support groups. Things are starting to improve, we have taken bits of advice and support from all above and amalgamated many different approaches – one size never fits all as they say.

We recognise signs of red mist, give her time to cool down in her own space, we let her slam the door and swear and pretend to ignore as complaining adds fuel to the fire. If she gets angry we quickly withdraw, attempting to calm or make physical contact winds her up further. Certain hotspots in the house have had potential big throwing items put elsewhere, e.g. the Hoover never left out on the landing any more, bookcase not by her bedroom door, TV mounted higher on the wall. We try to also ignore smaller misdemeanours, giving more attention and praise than previously for positive behaviour. She finds verbal praise hard to take so Post-It notes and cards are used a lot, cards are treasured and put in her keepsake box or stuck to her wall. We try to always be consistent as a partnership and certain family "rules" are written down. She has a timetable for getting to school, a timetable for school, a timetable for getting to bed. She needed more structure and less unpredictability. She also has a statement at school now and is being treated for previously undiagnosed ADHD. She is going to a new club and has made some friends. We have found out more about her birth parents which has been shared with her.

Things do still flare up, and I still feel like I am walking on eggshells much of the time, but I have had no bruises for over a year and less things have been broken. Things are calmer for all and she is happier which makes us all happier.

A week ago she insisted on watching a programme – *Born Naughty* on TV. I watched it with her, although I often avoid these programmes. She watched carefully and made lots of comments and said, 'I know how they [the children] feel, I feel poorly after I get angry, I don't like it. I worry and that is why I get angry. I can't believe I used to be as bad as that – shocking. I feel better now we are all getting help.'

I feel somewhat concerned about writing this post due to the subject matter, as I know one day she will read my blog posts and I do not want her to be upset, that is partly why I write under a "pseudonym". However, I thought it was important to share and show that things can improve and change, hopefully permanently. At times I used to be in a very sad place feeling very isolated, I want others to know it is alright to share and ask for help, and I hope you get it. Organised help (and Twitter of course!) have made a big difference to me in particular and of course to my daughter.

She does still blow up, but it is now less frequently and involves less damage to all involved physically and emotionally.

Today I got a lovely card from her.

Just as I am posting this she has thrown her Kindle against her wardrobe and broken it.

© Mending Mum

The peaceful protester

By frogotter

7 April 2015

https://frogotter.wordpress.com

We were pretty excited about attending a course[1] on Non Violent Resistance. It was run by Adoption UK and had Peter Jakob speaking. Violence has become our biggest concern with the boys. Not really because they're getting worse, if anything they are getting better at handling their impulses. But, as they get larger and stronger, any violence at all starts to be a bit worrying. So, a day course about dealing with aggression without getting aggressive sounded perfect.

I'd already read a book about it, but I was concerned that it seemed aimed at parents of older children, and wasn't entirely applicable to us, yet. On the other hand, some of the ideas sounded different to things I've read in other books, and that was rather exciting!

So, we turned up hopeful, but not expecting much.

The first thing I always look for from an expert is what they suggest we do in the moment of a tantrum. And, here Jakob was refreshingly reassuring. He said: 'When all hell breaks loose, then all hell breaks loose'. Fundamentally, his opinion seems to be that during an "incident", you can't actually change the relationship nor do any therapeutic work. During an incident, the sole aim should be minimising risk. That was very reassuring. I have spent years worrying about what we do in those highly charged, sometimes scary, moments. Jakob says that I should stop trying to control the child, and focus on minimising risk.

Which brings us to the next thing he talked about: control. He suggested that traumatised children sometimes try to 'reduce every interaction to a power struggle'. Rather than advising us, as parents, to "win", Jakob suggested we try to notice when this occurs and avoid entering into power struggles at all. He

---

1   NB: This account talks about having attended a one-day course, which of course is very different from the actual therapy itself, which goes on over a longer period and includes one-to-one support from a therapist while parents attempt to put their ideas into practice.

suggested that it wouldn't be a disaster if our children did 'think they've won'. At first, I found that quite challenging to hear. After all, isn't it vital for me to teach my children that violence and aggression don't win? But, as I thought about it, I realised that sometimes, I am as desperate for control as the boys, and that's not helping anyone! I can maintain greater authority by staying in control of myself and letting these little power struggles go.

He talked about 'reconciliatory gestures', such as offering a cup of tea (as I noticed from his book, he does seem to be thinking of older children and young adults, rather than small children). He also talks about 'parental presence', suggesting that we should enter our children's worlds. His examples include talking to their friends and visiting the places they go. He also mentioned finding out about their interests and – briefly – entering the virtual worlds they're inhabiting. This wasn't about spying, he says that we should be open and tell people what we're doing.

'You don't need friends, you need a support network,' also rang very true for me. Jakob has some very specific ideas of ways to use this support network. He suggests that secrecy can perpetuate abusive situations. Parents can ask other adults to bear witness by telling them about incidents and asking them to mention their concerns to the child.

He suggested a structured approach to raising concerns: the adult should mention that they know of the behaviour and are concerned for the child and for the parent and for the important relationship that is being damaged; they should offer a listening ear and (for older children) a safe place to go when the child needs a break; they should finish on a positive note, sharing their pleasure in the child, or praising something suitable. It is a lot to ask of supporters! We haven't decided if we're going to make the request yet.

Fundamentally, Jakob's approach seems to be based on two main principles:

- We cannot control our children, we can only control ourselves

- We can, and should, recruit supporters to aid us in parenting

I found it heartening, I think because he was so clear in his opinion that, during an incident, it doesn't much matter what we do. I worry that it sounds lazy of me, but I am just so relieved to hear that someone doesn't condemn me for not being therapeutic in the really awful moments.

Jakob has more suggestions, which do seem a bit extreme for us at the moment, like holding a "sit in" in protest at particularly difficult behaviour.

Ultimately, I think the best thing I took from his talk was the reassurance that my power to affect my children hasn't vanished because I can't control them. It is a new way of thinking about parenting. I don't have to choose between stopping a behaviour or permitting it; I can choose to resist it instead, to state my objections and stand firm. I thought that it might feel absurd to try and draw lessons from political movements to parent my boys. But, when Jakob talked, it felt inspiring. Rather than choosing between the roles of victim or policeman, I have a new role of peaceful protester.

© frogotter

5

PARENTING MATTERS

This unique series provides expert knowledge about a range of children's health conditions, coupled with facts, figures and guidance presented in a straightforward and accessible style. Adopters and foster carers also describe what it is like to parent an affected child, "telling it like it is", sharing their parenting experiences and offering useful advice.

To find out more visit www.corambaaf.org.uk/bookshop

References

Boffey D (2014) 'Children's hyperactivity "is not a real disease", says US expert', The Observer, 30 March 2014

Children and Young People's Mental Health Taskforce (2015) *Future in Mind: Promoting, Protecting and Improving Our Children and Young People's Mental Health and Wellbeing*, London: Department of Health

First4Adoption (2015) *The Adoption Passport: A support guide for adopters*, London: First4Adoption, available at: www.first4adoption.org.uk/wp-content/uploads/2016/03/The-Adoption-Passport.pdf

Hammond S and Cooper N (2013) *Digital Life Story Work*, London: BAAF

Louis J and Ghate D for The Colebrook Centre for Evidence and Implementation (2015) *Adoption Support Fund: Learning from the prototype*, London: Department for Education

McNeish D and Scott S (2013) *What Works in Achieving Adoption for Looked After Children: An overview of evidence for the Coram/Barnardo's partnership*, London: Coram/Barnardo's, available at: www.barnardos.org.uk/coram_barnardos_evidence_review_on_adoption.pdf

National Institute for Health and Care Excellence (2015) *Attachment in Children and Young People who are Adopted from Care, in Care or at High Risk of Going into Care,* National Clinical Guideline, London: NICE

Pennington E (2012) *It Takes a Village to Raise a Child: Adoption UK survey on adoption support*, Oxfordshire: Adoption UK

Rushton, A and Upright, H (2011) *Enhancing Adoptive Parenting: A Parenting Programme for Use with New Adopters of Challenging Children*, London: BAAF

Ryan T and Walker R (2016) *Life Story Work: Why, what, how and when* (6th edn), London: CoramBAAF

Selwyn J, Meakings S and Wijedasa D (2015) *Beyond the Adoption Order: Challenges, interventions and adoption disruption*, London: BAAF